Crochet
Little
Heroes

Crochet *Little* Heroes

Twenty Amigurumi Dolls to Make and Inspire

ORSI FARKASVÖLGYI

B.E.S.
PUBLISHING

A Quarto Book.

This edition for the United States and Canada published in 2020 by Barron's Educational Series, Inc, an imprint of Peterson's Publishing, LLC

ISBN-13: 978-1-4380-8902-7

Library of Congress Control No applied for.

All inquiries should be addressed to:
Peterson's Publishing, LLC
4380 S. Syracuse Street, Suite 200
Denver, CO 80237-2624
www.petersonsbooks.com

This book was designed and produced by
Quarto Publishing
The Old Brewery
6 Blundell Street
London N7 9BH

Editor: Emma Harverson
Designer: Martina Calvio
Project photographer: Nicki Dowey
Technique illustrations: Kuo Kang Chen
Publisher: Samantha Warrington

Printed in Singapore

10 9 8 7 6 5 4 3 2 1

CONTENTS

INTRODUCTION

Hello, dear crochet friend, and welcome to the world of *Crochet Little Heroes*. In the pages of this book, you will find everything you need to recreate twenty iconic heroes with colorful yarns and a crochet hook.

In the Projects section, you will meet the twenty incredible women and men who have been chosen from the many contemporary and present-day heroes I admire. During the process of creating these dolls, I got to know every one of them on a deeper level. I became familiar not only with their art, inspiration, or creativity, but also their struggles in life, and the hard work it has taken to overcome them. I've had my personal favorites, my own heroes among them, long before writing this book—but during the months I focused on these amazing artists, athletes, activists, and public figures, I managed to fall in love with each and every one of them, as I always found something that took my breath away. From Josephine Baker's unwavering bravery during World War II and the persistence of Rosa Parks and Malala, to the pure, inevitable talent of Prince, Frida Kahlo, and Audrey Hepburn—most of these heroes were innovators and revolutionists in their field. They were ahead of their time in so many ways. But what makes them special for me, and perhaps for most of us, is that they all made a lasting difference.

In the Techniques section of the book, you will find all of the stitches and techniques needed to crochet your own heroes. Each project lists the yarn type with my color choices, but I would also encourage you to choose your very own favorite colors, or even yarn brand. When it comes to amigurumi, I always use 100% cotton yarn, but you can experiment with different types of yarn, for example, wool or acrylic.

So, grab a cup of coffee or tea, settle yourself comfortably, pick up your crochet hook, and recreate each of the heroes in this book. I hope they will bring joy and happiness to your life and, most of all, inspire you.

YOU WILL NEED

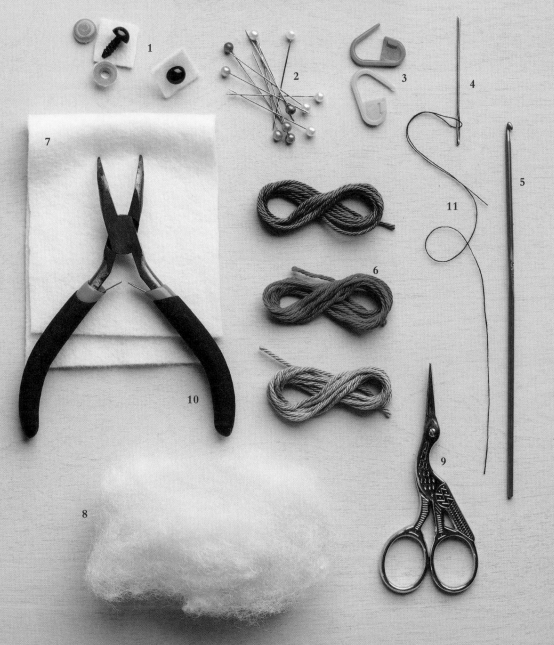

1. 5⁄16" (8mm) safety eyes **2.** Pins **3.** Stitch markers **4.** Tapestry needle
5. B–1 or C–2 (2.5 mm) crochet hook **6.** 100% cotton yarn **7.** White felt
8. Polyfiber stuffing **9.** Scissors **10.** Round-nose pliers **11.** Black thread
(See note on page 119 on how tools, materials, and gauge will affect the size of the finished dolls.)

THE PROJECTS

Coco Chanel
page 26

Abraham Lincoln
page 102

Malala Yousafzai
page 60

Jane Goodall
page 56

Prince
page 90

Make your own

MISTY COPELAND

Misty Copeland is a ballet dancer for the American Ballet Theatre. Despite starting to learn ballet at the relatively late age of thirteen—and being challenged by her difference—Misty became the company's first African-American soloist for two decades. At the age of thirty-two, she also became the first African-American woman to be promoted to principal dancer at the Theatre. Behind success there is often pain and suffering, and it was no different for Misty. She overcame family difficulties, health issues, and body-image struggles and went on to become a role model and pop icon.

MATERIALS

B-1 or C-2 (2.5 mm) crochet hook

5/16" (8 mm) safety eyes

Tapestry needle

Polyester fiberfill

Black thread for embroidery

Small amount of white felt

YARNS

Scheepjes Catona 100% cotton yarn:

507 Chocolate—skin, 20 g

105 Bridal White—dress, headpieces, 22 g

263 Petal Peach—shoes, 3 g

110 Jet Black—hair, 18 g

HEAD

Start with the skin color.

Rnd 1. 6 sc into magic ring (6).

Rnd 2. 2 sc into each (12).

Rnd 3. {sc, inc} 6 times (18).

Rnd 4. {sc into 2, inc} 6 times (24).

Rnd 5. {sc into 3, inc} 6 times (30).

Rnd 6. {sc into 4, inc} 6 times (36).

Rnd 7. {sc into 5, inc} 6 times (42).

Rnd 8. {sc into 6, inc} 6 times (48).

Rnd 9. {sc into 7, inc} 6 times (54).

Rnds 10–16. Sc into each (54).

Rnd 17. {sc into 8, inc} 6 times (60).

Rnds 18–20. Sc into each (60).

Rnd 21. {sc into 8, dec} 6 times (54).

Rnd 22. {sc into 7, dec} 6 times (48).

Rnd 23. {sc into 6, dec} 6 times (42).

Rnd 24. {sc into 5, dec} 6 times (36).

Add the eyes (see page 126 for guidance).

Rnd 25. {sc into 4, dec} 6 times (30).

Rnd 26. {sc into 3, dec} 6 times (24).

Start to stuff the head.

Rnd 27. {sc into 2, dec} 6 times (18).

Rnd 28. {sc, dec} 6 times (12).

Continue to stuff the head firmly.

Rnd 29. Sc into each FLO (12).

Do not fasten off, continue with the body.

BODY

Rnd 1. {sc, inc} 6 times (18).

Rnd 2. {sc into 2, inc} 6 times (24).

Change to the color of the dress.

Rnd 3. Sc into each (24).

Rnd 4. {sc into 3, inc} 6 times (30).

Rnd 5. Sc into each (30).

Rnd 6. {sc into 4, inc} 6 times (36).

Rnds 7–10. Sc into each (36).

Rnd 11. Sc into each BLO (36).

Rnd 12. Sc into each (36).

Rnd 13. {sc into 16, dec} 2 times (34).

Rnds 14–15. Sc into each (34).

Do not fasten off, continue with the legs. Stuff the neck and body continuously.

LEGS

To make the legs, divide the work: 14 stitches for each of the legs, and 3 stitches between the legs, both front and back. Mark the stitches with yarn or a stitch marker. Make sure the legs line up with the eyes. If the last stitch of the body is within the 14 stitches for the legs, then continue crocheting. If it is within the 3 stitches, then fasten off, leave a tail for sewing later, and rejoin the dress-colored yarn with a sl st at the back of the doll.

Rnds 1–3. Sc into each (14).

Rnd 4. {sc into 5, dec} 2 times (12).

Rnds 5–6. Sc into each (12).

Stuff the body firmly and stuff the leg as you crochet it.

Rnd 7. {sc into 4, dec} 2 times (10).

Rnds 8–12. Sc into each (10).

Stuff the leg firmly.

Rnd 13. Dec 5 times (5).

Fasten off, sew up the small hole, and weave in the ends. For the second leg, rejoin with a sl st at the back of the doll and work the leg. When finished, sew up the hole between the legs. Weave in the ends.

EYEBROWS AND NOSE

Using black thread, embroider the eyebrows between rounds 12 and 14. With skin-colored yarn, embroider the nose between rounds 18 and 19.

SKIRT

Using the color of the dress, join with a sl st to a front loop of round 10 at the center back of the body. Work continuously but join with a sl st at the end of each round. Ch 2 at the beginning does not count as dc.

Rnd 1. Ch 2, 2 dc into each. Join with a sl st to first dc (72).

Rnd 2. Ch 2, dc into each. Join with a sl st to first dc (72).

Rnd 3. Sl st into each (72).

Fasten off and weave in the ends.

HAIR

Use the hair color.

Rnd 1. 6 sc into magic ring (6).

Rnd 2. 2 sc into each (12).

Rnd 3. {sc, inc} 6 times (18).

Rnd 4. {sc into 2, inc} 6 times (24).

Rnd 5. {sc into 3, inc} 6 times (30).

Rnd 6. {sc into 4, inc} 6 times (36).

Rnd 7. {sc into 5, inc} 6 times (42).

Rnd 8. {sc into 6, inc} 6 times (48).

Rnd 9. {sc into 7, inc} 6 times (54).

Rnds 10–19. Sc into each (54).

Fasten off and leave a long tail for sewing. Place the hair on the head, secure it with pins, and sew it into place.

BUN

Use the hair color.

Rnd 1. 6 sc into magic ring (6).

Rnd 2. 2 sc into each (12).

Rnd 3. {sc, inc} 6 times (18).

Rnd 4. {sc into 2, inc} 6 times (24).

Rnds 5–7. Sc into each (24).

Rnd 8. {sc into 2, dec} 6 times (18).

Fasten off and leave a long tail for sewing. Stuff the bun, then place it on the head between rounds 2 and 8 of the hair. Secure the bun with pins, and sew it into place.

ARMS

Use the skin color, make two.

Rnd 1. 6 sc into magic ring (6).

Rnd 2. {sc, inc} 3 times (9).

Rnd 3. Sc into each (9).

Rnd 4. {sc, dec} 3 times (6).

Rnds 5–11. Sc into each (6).

Fasten off and leave a long tail for sewing. Sew an arm on each side of the doll and weave in the ends.

SHOES

Use the color of the shoes, make two.

Rnd 1. 6 sc into magic ring (6).

Rnd 2. 2 sc into each (12).

Rnds 3–4. Sc into each (12).

Fasten off and leave a long tail. Place one shoe onto a leg, ensuring the long tail is on the left. Cross the tail in front of the leg upward, and using a needle, pull the yarn through a stitch at round 7 at the back. Cross the tail in front of the leg downward, and insert the needle through the shoe and the leg from right to left. Secure the shoe with a few stitches. Fasten off and weave in the ends. Sew the second shoe to the other leg in the same way.

HEADPIECES

Use the color of the headpieces, make two.

Ch 10 (foundation chain), sl st into 2nd ch from hook and into next 2. ★ Ch 4, sl st into 2nd ch from hook and into next 2, sl st into next st on foundation chain. Repeat from ★ 6 times. Fasten off, leaving a long tail. Sew headpiece onto the hair at round 16 on one side of the head. Repeat for the other side. Weave in the ends.

Make your own

FRIDA KAHLO

Mexican artist Frida Kahlo was renowned for her self-portraits and use of vibrant colors. One of the most iconic women of the twentieth century, she is symbolic of love, passion, strength, suffering, and, most of all, art. A beautiful soul who lived her life to the fullest—displaying a deep sense of independence, rebellion, and outspoken political activism—Frida is still admired as a feminist icon today.

MATERIALS

B-1 or C-2 (2.5 mm) crochet hook

5⁄16" (8 mm) safety eyes

Tapestry needle

Polyester fiberfill

Black thread for embroidery

Extra fine merino wool—black

Small amount of white felt

YARNS

Scheepjes Catona 100% cotton yarn:

502 Camel—skin, 20 g

252 Watermelon—dress, 18 g

110 Jet Black—hair, 15 g

192 Scarlet—roses, 5 g

HEAD

Start with the skin color.

Rnd 1. 6 sc into magic ring (6).

Rnd 2. 2 sc into each (12).

Rnd 3. {sc, inc} 6 times (18).

Rnd 4. {sc into 2, inc} 6 times (24).

Rnd 5. {sc into 3, inc} 6 times (30).

Rnd 6. {sc into 4, inc} 6 times (36).

Rnd 7. {sc into 5, inc} 6 times (42).

Rnd 8. {sc into 6, inc} 6 times (48).

Rnd 9. {sc into 7, inc} 6 times (54).

Rnds 10–16. Sc into each (54).

Rnd 17. {sc into 8, inc} 6 times (60).

Rnds 18–20. Sc into each (60).

Rnd 21. {sc into 8, dec} 6 times (54).

Rnd 22. {sc into 7, dec} 6 times (48).

Rnd 23. {sc into 6, dec} 6 times (42).

Rnd 24. {sc into 5, dec} 6 times (36).

Add the eyes (see page 126 for guidance).

Rnd 25. {sc into 4, dec} 6 times (30).

Rnd 26. {sc into 3, dec} 6 times (24).

Start to stuff the head.

Rnd 27. {sc into 2, dec} 6 times (18).

Rnd 28. {sc, dec} 6 times (12).

Continue to stuff the head firmly.

Rnd 29. Sc into each FLO (12).

Change to the color of the dress.

BODY

From round 2 crochet into BLO throughout the body.

Rnd 1. {sc, inc} 6 times (18).

Rnd 2. BLO {sc into 2, inc} 6 times (24).

Rnd 3. BLO sc into each (24).

Rnd 4. BLO {sc into 3, inc} 6 times (30).

Rnds 5–6. BLO sc into each (30).

Rnd 7. BLO {sc into 4, inc} 6 times (36).

Rnds 8–9. BLO sc into each (36).

Rnd 10. BLO {sc into 5, inc} 6 times (42).

Rnds 11–15. BLO sc into each (42).

Rnd 16. BLO {sc into 5, dec} 6 times (36).

Start to stuff the neck and body continuously.

Rnd 17. BLO sc into each (36).

Rnd 18. BLO {sc into 4, dec} 6 times (30).

Rnd 19. BLO {sc into 3, dec} 6 times (24).

Rnd 20. BLO {sc into 2, dec} 6 times (18).

Stuff the body firmly.

Rnd 21. BLO {sc, dec} 6 times (12).

Rnd 22. BLO dec 6 times (6).

Fasten off and leave a long tail for sewing. Sew up the hole and weave in the ends.

EYEBROWS AND NOSE

Position two pins for the nose placement between rounds 18 and 19, and embroider the nose with skin-colored yarn. For the eyebrows, place five pins between rounds 12 and 13. Follow the pictures to place the pins and embroider the eyebrows with black thread. Embroider a "V" shape directly above the nose. You can add a cheek blush with makeup or watercolor pencil.

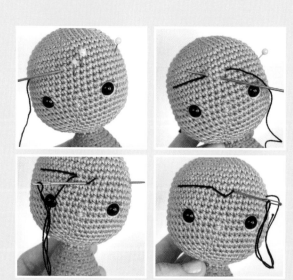

HAIR

Use the hair color.

Rnd 1. 6 sc into magic ring (6).

Rnd 2. 2 sc into each (12).

Rnd 3. {sc, inc} 6 times (18).

Rnd 4. {sc into 2, inc} 6 times (24).

Rnd 5. {sc into 3, inc} 6 times (30).

Rnd 6. {sc into 4, inc} 6 times (36).

Rnd 7. {sc into 5, inc} 6 times (42).

Rnd 8. {sc into 6, inc} 6 times (48).

Rnd 9. {sc into 7, inc} 6 times (54).

Rnds 10–17. Sc into each (54).

Rnd 18. Sc into 45, hdc into 7, sl st into 2 (54).

Rnd 19. Hdc into 7, sl st into 2.

Fasten off and leave a long tail for sewing. Place the hair on the head, secure it with pins, and sew it into place.

BRAID

Using three pieces of black merino wool, make a braid about 10" (25 cm) long. Place it around the head, secure it with pins, and using small stitches, sew it onto the hair.

ROSES

Use the color of the roses, make four.

Ch 11, turn, 2 sc into 2nd ch from hook and into next 9 (20). Fasten off and leave a long tail for sewing. Roll up and sew the bottom edges together with a few stitches. Place the roses onto the hair and sew into position.

LEGS

Start with the color of the dress, make two.

Rnd 1. 6 sc into magic ring (6).

Rnd 2. BLO 2 sc into each (12).

Rnd 3. BLO {sc into 2, inc} 4 times (16).

Rnds 4–5. BLO sc into each (16).

Rnd 6. BLO {sc into 2, dec} 4 times (12).

Rnd 7. BLO sc into each (12).

Change to the skin color.

Rnd 8. BLO sc into each (12).

Rnds 9–11. Sc into each (12).

Rnd 12. Inc 2 times, sc into 10 (14).

Rnd 13. Inc 4 times, sc into 10 (18).

Rnds 14–15. Sc into each (18).

Start to stuff the leg.

Rnd 16. Dec 9 times (9).

Rnd 17. Dec 3 more times.

Stuff the toe of the leg. Fasten off and leave a long tail for sewing. Sew up the hole and weave in the ends. Position a leg on each side of the doll and sew them into place.

DRESS EMBROIDERY

Using black thread, embroider three flowers onto the front of the dress. You will use basic stitches for the stems and French knots for the blossoms. Pull the needle through between rounds 14 and 15 of the body, and then thread it through four front loops, working upward and to the left in a straight line. Then, working downward, pull the needle from right to left through each black stitch between the front loops of the body. Do this all the way down to produce a black line. Then insert the needle into the starting point and pull it back out at the top of the stem. Mark the places for the offshoots with three pins and embroider them continuously. Position a French knot (see page 18) at the end of each offshoot. Do not fasten off after each flower; instead continue to embroider the middle and final flowers onto the dress in the same way.

Dress embroidery

FRENCH KNOTS

1. Pull the needle through to the front of the crochet where you want to place the French knot.

2. Holding your needle in one hand, use your other hand to wrap the thread around the needle 2 times, keeping the thread as taut as possible.

3. Insert the needle back into the crochet fabric (while holding the thread tightly) as close to your original starting point as possible, and pull the needle and the thread through to the next marker—while holding the thread taut. Try to avoid using the same hole because you will pull the knot through to the wrong side.

ARMS

Start with the color of the dress, make two.

Rnd 1. 6 sc into magic ring (6).

Rnd 2. BLO {sc, inc} 3 times (9).

Rnd 3. BLO {sc into 2, inc} 3 times (12).

Rnd 4. BLO sc into each (12).

Rnd 5. BLO {sc, dec} 4 times (8).

Rnd 6. BLO sc into each (8).

Slightly stuff the upper part of the arms. Change to the skin color.

Rnd 7. BLO sc into each (8).

Rnds 8–11. Sc into each (8).

Rnd 12. {sc into 2, inc} 2 times, sc into last 2 (10).

Rnds 13–14. Sc into each (10).

Rnd 15. Dec 5 times (5).

Fasten off and leave a long tail for sewing. Sew up the hole and weave in the ends. Position an arm on each side of the doll and sew them into place.

Make your own

RITA MORENO

Rita Moreno is a Puerto Rican actress, dancer, and singer. What's not to love about a woman who said Marlon Brando was the "lust of her life"? She is one of the few artists to have won all four major American entertainment awards: an Emmy, a Grammy, an Oscar, and a Tony. She was the first Latina actress to win an Oscar for her performance in *West Side Story*. In her nearly seventy-year career, Moreno has never stopped fighting against typecasting and for fair representation of Latinos. She returned to the stage aged eighty with her biographical one-woman show, which became a Broadway sensation.

MATERIALS

B-1 or C-2 (2.5 mm) crochet hook

⁵⁄₁₆" (8 mm) safety eyes

Tapestry needle

Polyester fiberfill

Black thread for embroidery

Small amount of white felt

YARNS

Scheepjes Catona 100% cotton yarn:

505 Linen—skin, 22 g

110 Jet Black—dress, gloves, 25 g

162 Black Coffee—hair, 20 g

383 Ginger Gold—flowers, shoes, 20 g

HEAD

Start with the skin color.

Rnd 1. 6 sc into magic ring (6).

Rnd 2. 2 sc into each (12).

Rnd 3. {sc, inc} 6 times (18).

Rnd 4. {sc into 2, inc} 6 times (24).

Rnd 5. {sc into 3, inc} 6 times (30).

Rnd 6. {sc into 4, inc} 6 times (36).

Rnd 7. {sc into 5, inc} 6 times (42).

Rnd 8. {sc into 6, inc} 6 times (48).

Rnd 9. {sc into 7, inc} 6 times (54).

Rnds 10–16. Sc into each (54).

Rnd 17. {sc into 8, inc} 6 times (60).

Rnds 18–20. Sc into each (60).

Rnd 21. {sc into 8, dec} 6 times (54).

Rnd 22. {sc into 7, dec} 6 times (48).

Rnd 23. {sc into 6, dec} 6 times (42).

Rnd 24. {sc into 5, dec} 6 times (36).

Add the eyes (see page 126 for guidance).

Rnd 25. {sc into 4, dec} 6 times (30).

Rnd 26. {sc into 3, dec} 6 times (24).

Start to stuff the head.

Rnd 27. {sc into 2, dec} 6 times (18).

Rnd 28. {sc, dec} 6 times (12).

Continue to stuff the head firmly.

Rnd 29. Sc into each FLO (12).

Change to the color of the dress.

BODY

Rnd 1. {sc, inc} 6 times (18).

Rnd 2. {sc into 2, inc} 6 times (24).

Rnd 3. Sc into each (24).

Rnd 4. {sc into 3, inc} 6 times (30).

Rnd 5. Sc into each (30).

Rnd 6. {sc into 4, inc} 6 times (36).

Rnds 7–9. Sc into each (36).

Rnd 10. Sc into each BLO (36).

Rnds 11–12. Sc into each (36).

Rnd 13. {sc into 16, dec} 2 times (34).

Rnds 14–15. Sc into each (34).

Fasten off and weave in the ends. Stuff the neck and body continuously.

LEGS

To make the legs, divide the work: 14 stitches for each of the legs, and 3 stitches between the legs, both front and back. Mark the stitches with yarn or a stitch marker. Make sure the legs line up with the eyes. Use skin-colored yarn and join with a sl st at the back of the doll to start.

Rnds 1–3. Sc into each (14).

Rnd 4. {sc into 5, dec} 2 times (12).

Rnds 5–8. Sc into each (12).

Stuff the body firmly and stuff the leg as you crochet it.

Rnd 9. {sc into 4, dec} 2 times (10).

Rnds 10–12. Sc into each (10).

Stuff the leg firmly.

Rnd 13. Dec 5 times (5).

Fasten off, sew up the small hole, and weave in the ends. For the second leg, rejoin with a sl st at the back of the doll and work the leg. When finished, use black yarn to sew up the hole between the legs. Weave in the ends.

SKIRT

Using the color of the dress, join with a sl st to a front loop of round 9 at the center back of the body. Work continuously but join with a sl st at the end of each round. Ch 1 at the beginning does not count as sc.

Rnd 1. Ch 1, {sc, inc} 18 times (54).

Rnds 2–17. Ch 1, sc into each (54).

Rnd 18. Ch 1, {hdc, inc} 27 times (81).

Rnd 19. Sl st into each (81).

Fasten off and weave in the ends.

EYEBROWS AND NOSE

Using black thread, embroider the eyebrows between rounds 12 and 14. With skin-colored yarn, embroider the nose between rounds 18 and 19. You can add a cheek blush with makeup or watercolor pencil.

FLOWERS

Use the color of the flowers, make six.

Rnd 1. 12 dc into magic ring (12).

Rnd 2. {ch 1, sl st into next} 12 times.

Fasten off and leave a long tail for sewing. Evenly space the flowers on the skirt, pin, and sew them into place. Embroider lines, 13/16" (2 cm) long, between the flowers. Embroider three dots on both sides of the lines using French knots (see page 18).

HAIR

Use the hair color.

Rnd 1. 6 sc into magic ring (6).

Rnd 2. 2 sc into each (12).

Rnd 3. {sc, inc} 6 times (18).

Rnd 4. {sc into 2, inc} 6 times (24).

Rnd 5. {sc into 3, inc} 6 times (30).

Rnd 6. {sc into 4, inc} 6 times (36).

Rnd 7. {sc into 5, inc} 6 times (42).

Rnd 8. {sc into 6, inc} 6 times (48).

Rnd 9. {sc into 7, inc} 6 times (54).

Rnds 10–16. Sc into each (54).

Rnd 17. Dc into 20, sc into next, sl st into next, ch 9, sl st into 2nd ch from hook and next 7, sl st into next on the wig. ★ Ch 7, sl st into 2nd ch from hook and next 5, sl st into next on the wig. Repeat from ★ 9 times. Ch 9, sl st into 2nd ch from hook and next 7, sl st into next on the wig. Sc into next on the wig, dc into last 20 on the wig. Fasten off and leave a long tail for sewing. Place the hair on the head, secure it with pins, and sew it into place.

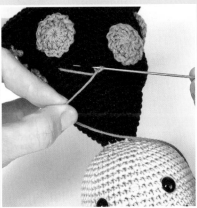

BUN

Use the hair color.

Rnd 1. 6 sc into magic ring (6).

Rnd 2. 2 sc into each (12).

Rnd 3. {sc, inc} 6 times (18).

Rnd 4. {sc into 2, inc} 6 times (24).

Rnd 5. {sc into 3, inc} 6 times (30).

Rnd 6. {sc into 4, inc} 6 times (36).

Rnds 7–9. Sc into each (36).

Rnd 10. {sc into 4, dec} 6 times (30).

Fasten off and leave a long tail for sewing. Stuff the bun, then place it on the head between rounds 6 and 17 of the hair. Secure the bun with pins, and sew it into place.

SHOES

Use the color of the shoes, make two.

Rnd 1. Ch 4, 2 sc into 2nd ch from hook, sc, 3 sc into next. Continue working on the other side of the foundation chain: sc, 2 sc into last (9).

Rnd 2. Inc 2 times, sc, inc 3 times, sc, inc 2 times (16).

Rnd 3. Sc into each BLO (16).

Rnd 4. Sc into 5, dec 3 times, sc into 5 (13).

Rnd 5. Sc into 6, dec, sc into 5 (12).

Fasten off and leave a long tail for sewing. Add stuffing to the toe of the shoes, position them on the legs, and sew them into place. Weave in the ends.

ARMS

Start with the color of the gloves, make two.

Rnd 1. 6 sc into magic ring (6).

Rnd 2. {sc, inc} 3 times (9).

Rnd 3. Sc into each (9).

Rnd 4. {sc, dec} 3 times (6).

Rnds 5–8. Sc into each (6).

Change to the skin color.

Rnd 9. Sc into each BLO (6).

Rnds 10–12. Sc into each (6).

Fasten off and leave a long tail for sewing. Position an arm on each side of the doll and sew them into place. Weave in the ends.

Make your own

COCO CHANEL

Gabrielle "Coco" Chanel was a French fashion designer and businesswoman. Regarded as an entrepreneur and polymath, a lesser known fact about her is that she designed the double-C logo for her brand—a logo that has been in use since the 1920s. She is admired and loved for several reasons. She was an innovator, establishing a new standard of style that liberated women from corsets; she founded the famous casual-chic style; and she invented the little black dress, the Chanel suit, and the iconic fragrance, Chanel No. 5.

MATERIALS

B-1 or C-2 (2.5 mm) crochet hook

⁵⁄₁₆" (8 mm) safety eyes

Tapestry needle

Polyester fiberfill

Black thread for embroidery

Small amount of white felt

YARNS

Scheepjes Catona 100% cotton yarn:

130 Old Lace—skin, 22 g

110 Jet Black—hair, skirt, 25 g

106 Snow White—shirt, 5 g

164 Light Navy—shirt, 10 g

502 Camel—hat, shoes, 10 g

HEAD

Start with the skin color.

Rnd 1. 6 sc into magic ring (6).

Rnd 2. 2 sc into each (12).

Rnd 3. {sc, inc} 6 times (18).

Rnd 4. {sc into 2, inc} 6 times (24).

Rnd 5. {sc into 3, inc} 6 times (30).

Rnd 6. {sc into 4, inc} 6 times (36).

Rnd 7. {sc into 5, inc} 6 times (42).

Rnd 8. {sc into 6, inc} 6 times (48).

Rnd 9. {sc into 7, inc} 6 times (54).

Rnds 10–16. Sc into each (54).

Rnd 17. {sc into 8, inc} 6 times (60).

Rnds 18–20. Sc into each (60).

Rnd 21. {sc into 8, dec} 6 times (54).

Rnd 22. {sc into 7, dec} 6 times (48).

Rnd 23. {sc into 6, dec} 6 times (42).

Rnd 24. {sc into 5, dec} 6 times (36).

Add the eyes (see page 126 for guidance).

Rnd 25. {sc into 4, dec} 6 times (30).

Rnd 26. {sc into 3, dec} 6 times (24).

Start to stuff the head.

Rnd 27. {sc into 2, dec} 6 times (18).

Rnd 28. {sc, dec} 6 times (12).

Continue to stuff the head firmly.

Rnd 29. Sc into each FLO (12).

Change to the blue shirt yarn.

BODY

Work continuously, but join with a sl st into the first st at the end of each round. Start with the blue yarn and change color at the end of each round.

Rnd 1. {sc, inc} 6 times (18). Change to white.

Rnd 2. {sc into 2, inc} 6 times (24). Change to blue.

Rnd 3. Sc into each (24). Change to white.

Rnd 4. {sc into 3, inc} 6 times (30). Change to blue.

Rnd 5. Sc into each (30). Change to white.

Rnd 6. {sc into 4, inc} 6 times (36). Change to blue.

Rnd 7. Sc into each (36). Change to white.

Rnd 8. Sc into each (36). Change to blue.

Rnd 9. Sc into each (36). Change to white.

Rnd 10. Sc into each (36).

Change to blue, fasten off white.

Rnd 11. Sc into each BLO (36).

Rnd 12. Sc into each (36).

Rnd 13. {sc into 16, dec} 2 times (34).

Rnds 14–15. Sc into each (34).

Fasten off and weave in the ends. Stuff the neck and body continuously.

LEGS

To make the legs, divide the work: 14 stitches for each of the legs, and 3 stitches between the legs, both front and back. Mark the stitches with yarn or a stitch marker. Make sure the legs line up with the eyes. Use skin-colored yarn and join with a sl st at the back of the doll to start.

Rnds 1–3. Sc into each (14).

Rnd 4. {sc into 5, dec} 2 times (12).

Rnds 5–8. Sc into each (12).

Stuff the body firmly and stuff the leg as you crochet it.

Rnd 9. {sc into 4, dec} 2 times (10).

Rnds 10–12. Sc into each (10).

Stuff the leg firmly.

Rnd 13. Dec 5 times (5).

Fasten off, sew up the small hole, and weave in the ends. For the second leg, rejoin with a sl st at the back of the doll and work the leg. When finished, use blue yarn to sew up the hole between the legs. Weave in the ends.

SKIRT

Using the color of the skirt, join with a sl st to a front loop of round 10 at the center back of the body. Work continuously, but join with a sl st at the end of each round. Ch 1 at the beginning does not count as sc.

Rnd 1. Ch 1, {sc into 2, inc} 12 times (48).

Rnd 2. Ch 1, BLO sc into each (48).

Rnd 3. Ch 1, BLO {sc into 5, inc} 8 times (56).

Rnds 4–14. Ch 1, BLO sc into each (56).

Rnd 15. Ch 1, sl st into each (56).

Fasten off and weave in the ends.

Round 1, Skirt

EYEBROWS AND NOSE

Using black thread, embroider the eyebrows between rounds 12 and 14. With skin-colored yarn, embroider the nose between rounds 18 and 19. You can add a cheek blush with makeup or watercolor pencil.

SHOES

Use the color of the shoes, make two.

Rnd 1. Ch 4, 2 sc into 2nd ch from hook, sc, 3 sc into next. Continue working on the other side of the foundation chain: sc, 2 sc into last (9).

Rnd 2. Inc 2 times, sc, inc 3 times, sc, inc 2 times (16).

Rnd 3. Sc into each BLO (16).

Rnd 4. Sc into 5, dec 3 times, sc into 5 (13).

Rnd 5. Sc into 6, dec, sc into 5 (12).

Fasten off and leave a long tail for sewing. Add stuffing to the toe of the shoes, position them on the legs, and sew them into place. Weave in the ends.

HAIR

Use the hair color.

Rnd 1. 6 sc into magic ring (6).

Rnd 2. 2 sc into each (12).

Rnd 3. {sc, inc} 6 times (18).

Rnd 4. {sc into 2, inc} 6 times (24).

Rnd 5. {sc into 3, inc} 6 times (30).

Rnd 6. {sc into 4, inc} 6 times (36).

Rnd 7. {sc into 5, inc} 6 times (42).

Rnd 8. {sc into 6, inc} 6 times (48).

Rnd 9. {sc into 7, inc} 6 times (54).

Rnds 10–11. Sc into each (54).

Rnd 12. Hdc into 8, sc into 8, hdc into 8, sc into 10, hdc into 8, sc into 4, hdc into 4, sc into 4 (54).

Rnd 13. Hdc into 10, sc into 5, hdc into 10, sc into 8, hdc into 10, sc into 2, hdc into 6, sc into 3 (54).

Rnd 14. Hdc into 8, sc into 8, hdc into 8, sc into 10, hdc into 8, sc into 3, hdc into 5, sc into 4 (54).

Rnd 15. Hdc into 8, sc into 8, hdc into 3, 3 hdc into next, hdc into 4, sc into 10, hdc into 4, 3 hdc into next, hdc into 3, sc into 5, hdc into 4, sc into 3 (58).

Rnd 16. Hdc into 8, sc into 8, hdc into 3, 3 hdc into next, hdc into 6, sc into 10, hdc into 6, 3 hdc into next, hdc into 3, sc into 4, hdc into 4, sc into 4 (62).

Rnd 17. Hdc into 6, sc into 10, hdc into 3, 3 hdc into next, hdc into 3, sc into 20, hdc into 3, 3 hdc into next, hdc into 3, sc into 4, hdc into 4, sc into 2, sl st into 2 (66).

Rnd 18. Sl st into each (66).

Fasten off and leave a long tail for sewing. Place the hair on the head, secure it with pins, and sew it into place.

ARMS

Start with blue shirt yarn, make two.

Work in continuous rounds. From rounds 2 to 5, change color at the end of each round.

Rnd 1. 6 sc into magic ring (6).

Rnd 2. {sc, inc} 3 times (9). Change to white.

Rnd 3. Sc into each (9). Change to blue.

Rnd 4. Sc into each (9). Change to white.

Rnd 5. {sc into 2, dec} 2 times, sc into last (7).

Change to blue, fasten off white. Stuff the upper part of the arm slightly.

Rnd 6. Sc into each (7).

Change to skin color, fasten off blue.

Rnds 7–11. Sc into each (7).

Rnd 12. {sc, inc} 3 times, sc into last (10).

Rnd 13. Dec 5 times (5).

Fasten off and leave a long tail for sewing. Sew up the small hole and weave in the ends. Position an arm on each side of the doll and sew them into place.

HAT

Use the color of the hat.

Rnd 1. 7 sc into magic ring (7).

Rnd 2. 2 sc into each (14).

Rnd 3. {sc, inc} 7 times (21).

Rnd 4. {sc into 6, inc} 3 times (24).

Rnd 5. Sc into each BLO (24).

Rnds 6–7. Sc into each (24).

Rnd 8. {sc, inc} 12 times (36).

Rnd 9. Sc into each (36).

Rnd 10. Sl st into each (36).

Fasten off and weave in the ends. With the same yarn, sew the hat onto the left side of the head.

Make your own

JOSEPHINE BAKER

Josephine Baker was an American-born French entertainer and civil rights activist. After a few years of dancing in New York City, she moved to Paris at the age of nineteen and became the most famous American performer in France. She revolutionized onstage performance with her erotic dancing and unusual costumes, and was also known for having a pet cheetah named Chiquita. She was multitalented, recognized not only for her dancing, but also for singing and acting. During World War II she worked with the French Resistance, and later became involved with the American civil rights movement. Ernest Hemingway called her "the most sensational woman anyone ever saw."

MATERIALS

B-1 or C-2 (2.5 mm) crochet hook

5⁄16" (8 mm) safety eyes

Tapestry needle

Polyester fiberfill

Black thread for embroidery

Small amount of white felt

YARNS

Scheepjes Catona 100% cotton yarn:

507 Chocolate—skin, 25 g

522 Primrose—dress, 15 g

110 Jet Black—hair, shoes, 18 g

HEAD

Start with the skin color.

Rnd 1. 6 sc into magic ring (6).

Rnd 2. 2 sc into each (12).

Rnd 3. {sc, inc} 6 times (18).

Rnd 4. {sc into 2, inc} 6 times (24).

Rnd 5. {sc into 3, inc} 6 times (30).

Rnd 6. {sc into 4, inc} 6 times (36).

Rnd 7. {sc into 5, inc} 6 times (42).

Rnd 8. {sc into 6, inc} 6 times (48).

Rnd 9. {sc into 7, inc} 6 times (54).

Rnds 10–16. Sc into each (54).

Rnd 17. {sc into 8, inc} 6 times (60).

Rnds 18–20. Sc into each (60).

Rnd 21. {sc into 8, dec} 6 times (54).

Rnd 22. {sc into 7, dec} 6 times (48).

Rnd 23. {sc into 6, dec} 6 times (42).

Rnd 24. {sc into 5, dec} 6 times (36).

Add the eyes (see page 126 for guidance).

Rnd 25. {sc into 4, dec} 6 times (30).

Rnd 26. {sc into 3, dec} 6 times (24).

Start to stuff the head.

Rnd 27. {sc into 2, dec} 6 times (18).

Rnd 28. {sc, dec} 6 times (12).

Continue to stuff the head firmly.

Rnd 29. Sc into each FLO (12).

Do not fasten off, continue with the body.

BODY

Rnd 1. {sc, inc} 6 times (18).

Rnd 2. {sc into 2, inc} 6 times (24).

Change to the color of the dress.

Rnd 3. Sc into each (24).

Rnd 4. BLO {sc into 3, inc} 6 times (30).

Rnd 5. BLO sc into each (30).

Rnd 6. BLO {sc into 4, inc} 6 times (36).

Change to the skin color.

Rnd 7. BLO sc into each (36).

Rnds 8–10. Sc into each (36).

Change to the color of the dress.

Rnd 11. Sc into each (36).

Rnd 12. BLO sc into each (36).

Rnd 13. BLO {sc into 16, dec} 2 times (34).

Rnds 14–15. BLO sc into each (34).

Fasten off and weave in the ends. Stuff the neck and body continuously.

LEGS

To make the legs, divide the work: 14 stitches for each of the legs, and 3 stitches between the legs, both front and back. Mark the stitches with yarn or a stitch marker. Make sure the legs line up with the eyes. Use skin-colored yarn and join with a sl st at the back of the doll to start.

Rnds 1–3. Sc into each (14).

Rnd 4. {sc into 5, dec} 2 times (12).

Rnds 5–8. Sc into each (12).

Stuff the body firmly and stuff the leg as you crochet it.

Rnd 9. {sc into 4, dec} 2 times (10).

Rnds 10–12. Sc into each (10).

Stuff the leg firmly.

Rnd 13. Dec 5 times (5).

Fasten off, sew up the small hole, and weave in the ends. For the second leg, rejoin with a sl st at the back of the doll and work the leg. When finished, use yellow yarn to sew up the hole between the legs. Weave in the ends.

EYEBROWS AND NOSE

Using black thread, embroider the eyebrows between rounds 12 and 14. With skin-colored yarn, embroider the nose between rounds 18 and 19.

SHOES

Use the color of the shoes, make two.

Rnd 1. Ch 4, 2 sc into 2nd ch from hook, sc, 3 sc into next. Continue working on the other side of the foundation chain: sc, 2 sc into last (9).

Rnd 2. Inc 2 times, sc, inc 3 times, sc, inc 2 times (16).

Rnd 3. Sc into each BLO (16).

Rnd 4. Sc into 5, dec 3 times, sc into 5 (13).

Rnd 5. Sc into 6, dec, sc into 5 (12).

Fasten off and leave a long tail for sewing. Add stuffing to the toe of the shoes, position them on the legs, and sew them into place. Weave in the ends.

SKIRT PETALS

Use the color of the dress, make nine.

Rnd 1. 6 sc into magic ring (6).

Rnd 2. {sc into 2, inc} 2 times (8).

Rnd 3. {sc into 3, inc} 2 times (10).

Rnds 4–6. Sc into each (10).

Rnd 7. {sc into 3, dec} 2 times (8).

Rnd 8. Sc into 2, sl st into next.

Fasten off and leave a long tail for sewing. Evenly space the petals on the first round of the panties, secure them with pins, and sew them into place.

ARMS

Use the skin color, make two.

Rnd 1. 6 sc into magic ring (6).

Rnd 2. {sc, inc} 3 times (9).

Rnd 3. Sc into each (9).

Rnd 4. {sc, dec} 3 times (6).

Rnds 5–12. Sc into each (6).

Fasten off and leave a long tail for sewing. Position an arm on each side of the doll and sew them into place.

HAIR

Use the hair color.

Rnd 1. 6 sc into magic ring (6).

Rnd 2. 2 sc into each (12).

Rnd 3. {sc, inc} 6 times (18).

Rnd 4. {sc into 2, inc} 6 times (24).

Rnd 5. {sc into 3, inc} 6 times (30).

Rnd 6. {sc into 4, inc} 6 times (36).

Rnd 7. {sc into 5, inc} 6 times (42).

Rnd 8. {sc into 6, inc} 6 times (48).

Rnd 9. {sc into 7, inc} 6 times (54).

Rnds 10–17. Sc into each (54).

Rnd 18. Sc, sl st into next 2, hdc into next 2, dc into next 40, hdc into next 4, ch 7, turn, sl st into 2nd ch from hook and into next, dec, sl st into next 2, 3 sc into next on the wig, hdc into next 3.

Rnd 19. Sc, sl st into next 2, hdc into next 7, ch 9, turn, sl st into 2nd ch from hook and into next, sc into next 2, hdc into next, sc into next 2, sl st into last of ch 9. Sc into next on the wig, sc into next 10, ch 6, turn, sl st into 2nd ch from hook and into next, sc into next 2, sl st into last of ch 6. Sc into next 2 on the wig, sl st into next 5.

Fasten off and leave a long tail for sewing. Place the hair on the head, secure it with pins, and sew it into place. Sew the locks onto the head.

Make your own

MAYA ANGELOU

Maya Angelou was an American autobiographer, poet, actress, screenwriter, dancer, composer, and activist. She is perhaps best known for her 1969 memoir *I Know Why the Caged Bird Sings*—the first nonfiction bestseller by an African-American woman. It was followed by six more autobiographies, several books of poetry, and essays. As a civil rights activist, she worked with Malcolm X and Dr. Martin Luther King, Jr.. Her *Georgia, Georgia* (1972) was the first feature film written by a black woman. As one of her husbands said, she accomplished more in a decade than many artists hope to achieve in a lifetime.

MATERIALS

B-1 or C-2 (2.5 mm) crochet hook

⁵⁄₁₆" (8 mm) safety eyes

Tapestry needle

Polyester fiberfill

Black thread for embroidery

Small amount of white felt

Fabric for the head wrap: 4½ x 17½" (11.5 x 45 cm)

Thread matching the fabric

YARNS

Scheepjes Catona 100% cotton yarn:

507 Chocolate—skin, 25 g

263 Petal Peach—panties, 4 g

408 Old Rose—dress, 18 g

164 Light Navy—dress, bow, 6 g

110 Jet Black—hair, shoes, 6 g

074 Mercury—hair, 2 g

HEAD

Start with the skin color.

Rnd 1. 6 sc into magic ring (6).

Rnd 2. 2 sc into each (12).

Rnd 3. {sc, inc} 6 times (18).

Rnd 4. {sc into 2, inc} 6 times (24).

Rnd 5. {sc into 3, inc} 6 times (30).

Rnd 6. {sc into 4, inc} 6 times (36).

Rnd 7. {sc into 5, inc} 6 times (42).

Rnd 8. {sc into 6, inc} 6 times (48).

Rnd 9. {sc into 7, inc} 6 times (54).

Rnds 10–16. Sc into each (54).

Rnd 17. {sc into 8, inc} 6 times (60).

Rnds 18–20. Sc into each (60).

Rnd 21. {sc into 8, dec} 6 times (54).

Rnd 22. {sc into 7, dec} 6 times (48).

Rnd 23. {sc into 6, dec} 6 times (42).

Rnd 24. {sc into 5, dec} 6 times (36).

Add the eyes (see page 126 for guidance).

Rnd 25. {sc into 4, dec} 6 times (30).

Rnd 26. {sc into 3, dec} 6 times (24).

Start to stuff the head.

Rnd 27. {sc into 2, dec} 6 times (18).

Rnd 28. {sc, dec} 6 times (12).

Continue to stuff the head firmly.

Rnd 29. Sc into each FLO (12).

Do not fasten off, continue with the body.

BODY

Rnd 1. BLO {sc into 2, inc} 4 times (16).

Rnd 2. {sc into 3, inc} 4 times (20).

Rnd 3. Sc into each (20).

Rnd 4. {sc into 4, inc} 4 times (24).

Rnd 5. Sc into each (24).

Rnd 6. {sc into 5, inc} 4 times (28).

Rnd 7. Sc into each (28).

Rnd 8. {sc into 6, inc} 4 times (32).

Rnd 9. {sc into 7, inc} 4 times (36).

Rnd 10. Sc into each (36).

Change to the color of the panties.

Rnds 11–12. Sc into each (36).

Rnd 13. {sc into 16, dec} 2 times (34).

Rnds 14–15. Sc into each (34).

Fasten off and weave in the ends. Stuff the neck and body continuously.

DRESS

Before continuing with the legs, crochet the dress. Using the color of the dress, join with a sl st to a front loop of round 29 at the center back of the head. Work continuously, but join with a sl st at the end of each round. Ch 2 at the beginning does not count as dc.

Rnd 1. {sc, inc} 6 times (18).

Rnd 2. Ch 2, 2 dc into each (36).

Rnd 3. Ch 2, {fpdc into next dc, bpdc into next dc} 18 times (36).

Rnds 4–5. Ch 2, {fpdc into prev rnd fpdc, bpdc into each of next 2 prev rnd bpdc} 18 times (36).

Rnd 6. Ch 2, {fpdc into prev rnd fpdc, 2 bpdc into prev rnd bpdc} 18 times (54).

Rnds 7–13. Ch 2, {fpdc into prev rnd fpdc, bpdc into each of next 2 prev rnd bpdc} 18 times (54).

Change to blue yarn.

Rnd 14. {(sc, dc, sc) into same st, sl st into next} 27 times. Fasten off and weave in the ends.

Round 3, Dress

LEGS

To make the legs, divide the work: 14 stitches for each of the legs, and 3 stitches between the legs, both front and back. Mark the stitches with yarn or a stitch marker. Make sure the legs line up with the eyes. Use skin-colored yarn and join with a sl st at the back of the doll to start.

Rnds 1–3. Sc into each (14).

Rnd 4. {sc into 5, dec} 2 times (12).

Rnds 5–8. Sc into each (12).

Stuff the body firmly and stuff the leg as you crochet it.

Rnd 9. {sc into 4, dec} 2 times (10).

Rnds 10–12. Sc into each (10). Stuff the legs firmly.

Rnd 13. Dec 5 times (5).

Fasten off, sew up the small hole, and weave in the ends. For the second leg, rejoin with a sl st at the back of the

doll and work the leg. When finished, use the peach yarn to sew up the hole between the legs. Weave in the ends.

ARMS

Start with the color of the dress, make two.

Rnd 1. 6 sc into magic ring (6).

Rnd 2. Inc 6 times (12).

Rnds 3–4. Sc into each (12).

Rnd 5. {sc, dec} 4 times (8).

Stuff the upper part of the arm slightly.

Rnds 6–12. Sc into each (8).

Change to the skin color.

Rnd 13. Sc into each BLO (8).

Rnd 14. {sc into 3, inc} 2 times (10).

Rnd 15. Sc into each (10).

Rnd 16. Dec 5 times (5).

Fasten off and leave a long tail for sewing. Sew the hole closed and weave in the ends. Position an arm on each side of the doll and sew them into place.

BOW

Use the blue yarn.

Row 1. Ch 9, sc into 2nd ch from hook and into next 7 (8).

Rows 2–5. Ch 1, sc into each BLO (8).

Fasten off and leave a long tail for sewing. Thread the tail into a needle and insert it through the top loops of the last row until you reach the center. Wrap the tail over a few times to make a nice center and sew the bow onto the dress.

SHOES

Use the color for the shoes, make two.

Rnd 1. Ch 4, 2 sc into 2nd ch from hook, sc, 3 sc into next. Continue working on the other side of the foundation chain: sc, 2 sc into last (9).

Rnd 2. Inc 2 times, sc, inc 3 times, sc, inc 2 times (16).

Rnd 3. Sc into each BLO (16).

Rnd 4. Sc into 5, dec 3 times, sc into 5 (13).
Rnd 5. Sc into 6, dec, sc into 5 (12).
Fasten off and leave a long tail for sewing. Add stuffing to
the toe of the shoes, position them on the legs, and sew
them into place. Weave in the ends.

EYEBROWS AND NOSE

Using black thread, embroider the eyebrows between
rounds 12 and 14. With skin-colored yarn, embroider the
nose between rounds 18 and 19.

HAIR AND HEAD WRAP

Make three locks with black yarn and one with gray yarn.
Ch 15, 2 sc into 2nd ch from hook and into each ch (28).
Fasten off and leave long tail for sewing. Place the locks
onto the head and sew them into place.

Place the doll's head into the middle of the fabric and tie a
knot at the top of the head. Arrange the ends neatly, secure
them with pins, and sew the ensemble onto the head with
matching thread.

Make your own

JANE AUSTEN

English novelist Jane Austen is world-renowned for her six major novels. As a young lady in eighteenth-century England, Jane was obsessed with books and was just eleven years old when she started to write poems and stories. Jane's timeless appeal is characterized by her humorous and satirical observations of eighteenth-century society. She was ahead of her time in the way she wrote about women, love, and marriage, and profoundly altered the sentimental narrative for girls—and we couldn't love her more for it!

MATERIALS

B-1 or C-2 (2.5 mm) crochet hook

⁵⁄₁₆" (8 mm) safety eyes

Tapestry needle

Polyester fiberfill

Black thread for embroidery

Small amount of white felt

YARNS

Scheepjes Catona 100% cotton yarn:

130 Old Lace—skin, 22 g

528 Silver Blue—dress (A), 18 g

403 Lemonade—dress (B), panties, 7 g

502 Camel—shoes, 3 g

507 Chocolate—hair, 18 g

HEAD

Start with the skin color.

Rnd 1. 6 sc into magic ring (6).

Rnd 2. 2 sc into each (12).

Rnd 3. {sc, inc} 6 times (18).

Rnd 4. {sc into 2, inc} 6 times (24).

Rnd 5. {sc into 3, inc} 6 times (30).

Rnd 6. {sc into 4, inc} 6 times (36).

Rnd 7. {sc into 5, inc} 6 times (42).

Rnd 8. {sc into 6, inc} 6 times (48).

Rnd 9. {sc into 7, inc} 6 times (54).

Rnds 10–16. Sc into each (54).

Rnd 17. {sc into 8, inc} 6 times (60).

Rnds 18–20. Sc into each (60).

Rnd 21. {sc into 8, dec} 6 times (54).

Rnd 22. {sc into 7, dec} 6 times (48).

Rnd 23. {sc into 6, dec} 6 times (42).

Rnd 24. {sc into 5, dec} 6 times (36).

Add the eyes (see page 126 for guidance).

Rnd 25. {sc into 4, dec} 6 times (30).

Rnd 26. {sc into 3, dec} 6 times (24).

Start to stuff the head.

Rnd 27. {sc into 2, dec} 6 times (18).

Rnd 28. {sc, dec} 6 times (12).

Continue to stuff the head firmly.

Rnd 29. Sc into each FLO (12).

Do not fasten off, continue with the body.

BODY

Rnd 1. {sc, inc} 6 times (18).

Rnd 2. {sc into 2, inc} 6 times (24).

Change to the color of the dress.

Rnd 3. Sc into each (24).

Rnd 4. {sc into 3, inc} 6 times (30).

Rnd 5. Sc into each (30).

Change to the skin color.

Rnd 6. Sc into each BLO (30).

Rnd 7. {sc into 4, inc} 6 times (36).

Rnds 8–9. Sc into each (36).

Rnd 10. {sc into 5, inc} 6 times (42).

Rnds 11–12. Sc into each (42).

Stuff the neck and body continuously.

Change to the color of the panties.

Rnds 13–15. Sc into each (42).

Rnd 16. {sc into 5, dec} 6 times (36).

Rnd 17. Sc into each (36).

Rnd 18. {sc into 4, dec} 6 times (30).

Rnd 19. {sc into 3, dec} 6 times (24).

Rnd 20. {sc into 2, dec} 6 times (18).

Stuff the body firmly.

Rnd 21. {sc, dec} 6 times (12).

Rnd 22. Dec 6 times (6).

Fasten off and leave a long tail for sewing. Sew up the hole and weave in the ends.

DRESS

Using dress color A (silver blue), join with a sl st to a front loop of round 5 at the center back of the body. Work continuously, but join with a sl st at the end of each round. Start rounds 1 to 5 with ch 2, which does not count as dc. Start rounds 6 to 7 with ch 1, which does not count as sc.

Rnd 1. Ch 2, {dc, inc} 15 times (45).

Rnd 2. Ch 2, {dc into 2, inc} 15 times (60).

Rnds 3–5. Ch 2, dc into each (60).

Rnd 6. Ch 1, FLO 3 hdc into each (180).

Fasten off and weave in the ends.

Rnd 7. With dress color B (yellow), join with a sl st into a back loop of round 5. Ch 1, BLO {sc, sk 1 st, 5 dc into next, sk 1 st} 15 times (15 shells).

Fasten off and weave in the ends.

EYEBROWS AND NOSE

Using black thread, embroider the eyebrows between rounds 12 and 14. With skin-colored yarn, embroider the nose between rounds 18 and 19. You can add a cheek blush with makeup or watercolor pencil.

HAIR

Use the hair color.

Rnd 1. 6 sc into magic ring (6).

Rnd 2. 2 sc into each (12).

Rnd 3. {sc, inc} 6 times (18).

Rnd 4. {sc into 2, inc} 6 times (24).

Rnd 5. {sc into 3, inc} 6 times (30).

Rnd 6. {sc into 4, inc} 6 times (36).

Rnd 7. {sc into 5, inc} 6 times (42).

Rnd 8. {sc into 6, inc} 6 times (48).

Rnd 9. {sc into 7, inc} 6 times (54).

Rnds 10–18. Sc into each (54). Do not fasten off,
sl st into next st.

Curl 1. Ch 8, 2 sc into 2nd ch from hook and next 6,
sl st into next 3 on the hair.

Curl 2. Repeat curl 1.

Curl 3. Ch 8, 2 sc into 2nd ch from hook and next 6,
sl st into next 18 on the hair.

Curls 4–6. Repeat curl 1.

Fasten off and leave a long tail for sewing. Place the hair
on the head, secure it with pins, and sew it into place.

BUN

Use the hair color.

Rnd 1. 6 sc into magic ring (6).

Rnd 2. 2 sc into each (12).

Rnd 3. {sc, inc} 6 times (18).

Rnd 4. {sc into 2, inc} 6 times (24).

Rnds 5–6. Sc into each (24).

Rnd 7. {sc into 2, dec} 6 times (18).

Rnd 8. {sc, dec} 6 times (12).

Fasten off and leave a long tail for sewing. Stuff the bun,
then place it on the head between rounds 1 and 6 of the
hair. Secure the bun with pins, and sew it into place.

ARMS

Start with the color of the dress, make two.

Rnd 1. 6 sc into magic ring (6).

Rnd 2. 2 sc into each (12).

Rnd 3. {sc, inc} 6 times (18).

Rnd 4. Sc into each (18).

Rnd 5. {sc, dec} 6 times (12).

Rnd 6. {sc, dec} 4 times (8).

Slightly stuff the dress part of the arms.

Change to the skin color.

Rnds 7–14. Sc into each (8).

Rnd 15. {sc into 2, inc} 2 times, sc into last 2 (10).

Rnd 16. Sc into each (10).

Rnd 17. Dec 5 times (5).

Fasten off and leave a long tail for sewing. Sew up the
hole and weave in the ends.

LEGS

Start with the skin color, make two.

Rnd 1. 6 sc into magic ring (6).

Rnd 2. 2 sc into each (12).

Rnd 3. {sc into 2, inc} 4 times (16).

Rnds 4–5. Sc into each (16).

Rnd 6. {sc into 2, dec} 4 times (12).

Rnds 7–12. Sc into each (12).

Rnd 13. Inc 2 times, sc into 10 (14).

Change to the color of the shoes.

Rnd 14. Inc 4 times, sc into 10 (18).

Rnds 15–16. Sc into each (18).

Rnd 17. Dec 9 times (9).

Start to stuff the leg.

Rnd 18. Dec 3 more times.

Stuff the toe of the leg. Fasten off and leave a long tail
for sewing. Sew up the hole and weave in the ends.
Position an arm and leg on each side of the doll and sew
them into place.

Make your own

BRUCE LEE

American-born Bruce Lee was a movie star, a cultural icon, and the most influential martial artist of the twentieth century. Alongside his lifelong dedication to practicing martial arts, Lee studied dramatic arts, philosophy, and psychology at college. He founded a martial arts academy to pass on what he had learned to students. Lee soon came to the attention of a Hollywood producer and quickly became a superstar. His four most legendary movies—*Fist of Fury, Enter the Dragon, The Way of the Dragon,* and *The Game of Death*—have been watched by millions and have made him a movie icon.

MATERIALS

B-1 or C-2 (2.5 mm) crochet hook

5/16" (8 mm) oval safety eyes

Tapestry needle

Polyester fiberfill

Black thread for embroidery

YARNS

Scheepjes Catona 100% cotton yarn:

505 Linen—skin, 20 g

522 Primrose—jumpsuit, 22 g

110 Jet Black—hair, shoes, stripes, 18 g

HEAD

Start with the skin color.

Rnd 1. 6 sc into magic ring (6).

Rnd 2. 2 sc into each (12).

Rnd 3. {sc, inc} 6 times (18).

Rnd 4. {sc into 2, inc} 6 times (24).

Rnd 5. {sc into 3, inc} 6 times (30).

Rnd 6. {sc into 4, inc} 6 times (36).

Rnd 7. {sc into 5, inc} 6 times (42).

Rnd 8. {sc into 6, inc} 6 times (48).

Rnd 9. {sc into 7, inc} 6 times (54).

Rnds 10–16. Sc into each (54).

Rnd 17. {sc into 8, inc} 6 times (60).

Rnds 18–20. Sc into each (60).

Rnd 21. {sc into 8, dec} 6 times (54).

Rnd 22. {sc into 7, dec} 6 times (48).

Rnd 23. {sc into 6, dec} 6 times (42).

Rnd 24. {sc into 5, dec} 6 times (36).

Add the eyes (see page 126 for guidance). Before placing them, use black thread to embroider two long horizontal stitches from the eye position outward.

Rnd 25. {sc into 4, dec} 6 times (30).

Rnd 26. {sc into 3, dec} 6 times (24).

Start to stuff the head.

Rnd 27. {sc into 2, dec} 6 times (18).

Rnd 28. {sc, dec} 6 times (12).

Continue to stuff the head firmly.

Rnd 29. Sc into each FLO (12).

Change to the color of the jumpsuit.

BODY

From round 2 crochet into BLO throughout the jumpsuit.

Rnd 1. {sc, inc} 6 times (18).

Rnd 2. BLO {sc into 2, inc} 6 times (24).

Rnd 3. BLO sc into each (24).

Rnd 4. BLO {sc into 3, inc} 6 times (30).

Rnd 5. BLO sc into each (30).

Rnd 6. BLO {sc into 4, inc} 6 times (36).

Rnds 7–12. BLO sc into each (36).

Rnd 13. BLO {sc into 16, dec} 2 times (34).

Rnd 14. BLO sc into each (34).

Do not fasten off, continue with the legs. Stuff the neck and body continuously.

LEGS

To make the legs, divide the work: 14 stitches for each of the legs, and 3 stitches between the legs, both front and back. Mark the stitches with yarn or a stitch marker. Make sure the legs line up with the eyes. If the last stitch of the body is within the 14 stitches for the legs, then continue crocheting. If it is within the 3 stitches, then fasten off, leave a tail for sewing later, and rejoin the jumpsuit-colored yarn with a sl st at the back of the doll.

Rnds 1–3. BLO sc into each (14).

Rnd 4. BLO {sc into 5, dec} 2 times (12).

Rnds 5–8. BLO sc into each (12).

Stuff the body firmly and stuff the leg as you crochet it.

Rnd 9. BLO {sc into 4, dec} 2 times (10).

Rnd 10. BLO sc into each (10).

Change to the skin color.

Rnd 11. BLO sc into each (10).

Rnd 12. Sc into each (10).

Stuff the leg firmly.

Rnd 13. Dec 5 times (5).

Fasten off, sew up the small hole, and weave in the ends. For the second leg, rejoin with a sl st at the back of the doll and work the leg. When finished, sew up the hole between the legs. Weave in the ends.

EYEBROWS AND NOSE

Using black thread, embroider the eyebrows between rounds 14 and 15, right above the eyes. With skin-colored yarn, embroider the nose between rounds 18 and 19.

JUMPSUIT EMBROIDERY

Using black yarn, pull the needle through between rounds 10 and 11 on the outside of the jumpsuit leg and then thread it through each front loop, working upward in a straight line until you reach the first round of the jumpsuit. Then, working downward, pull the needle from right to left through each black stitch between the front loops, all the way down. Fasten off and weave in the ends. Repeat on the other side of the doll and on the insides of the legs.

ARMS

Start with the skin color, make two.

Rnd 1. 6 sc into magic ring (6).

Rnd 2. {sc, inc} 3 times (9).

Rnd 3. Sc into each (9).

Rnd 4. {sc into 2, dec} 2 times, sc into last (7). Change to the color of the jumpsuit.

Rnd 5. Sc into each (7).

Rnds 6–13. Sc into each BLO.

Fasten off and leave a long tail for sewing. Embroider the black lines on the outside of both arms using the same method as for the stripes on the legs. Use small stitches to sew the arms onto the body.

SHOES

Use the color of the shoes, make two.

Rnd 1. Ch 4, 2 sc into 2nd ch from hook, sc, 3 sc into next. Continue working on the other side of the foundation chain: sc, 2 sc into last (9).

Rnd 2. Inc 2 times, sc, inc 3 times, sc, inc 2 times (16).

Rnd 3. Sc into each BLO (16).

Rnd 4. Sc into 5, dec 3 times, sc into 5 (13).

Rnd 5. Sc into 5, dec, sc into 6 (12).

Fasten off and leave a long tail for sewing. Add stuffing to the toe of the shoes, position them on the legs, and sew them into place. Weave in the ends.

HAIR

Use the hair color.

Rnd 1. 6 sc into magic ring (6).

Rnd 2. 2 sc into each (12).

Rnd 3. {sc, inc} 6 times (18).

Rnd 4. {sc into 2, inc} 6 times (24).

Rnd 5. {sc into 3, inc} 6 times (30).

Rnd 6. {sc into 4, inc} 6 times (36).

Rnd 7. {sc into 5, inc} 6 times (42).

Rnd 8. {sc into 6, inc} 6 times (48).

Rnd 9. {sc into 7, inc} 6 times (54).

Rnds 10–17. Sc into each (54).

Rnd 18. Sc into next, hdc into next, dc into next 4, hdc into next, sc into next 4, sl st into next, ★ ch 3, sl st into 2nd ch from hook and into next, sl st into next on the wig. Repeat from ★ 11 times. Sc into next 4, hdc into next, dc into next 4, hdc into next, sc into next 2, sl st into next, ★★ ch 4, sl st into 2nd ch from hook and into next 2, sl st into next on the wig. Repeat from ★★ 16 times. Sc into last.

Fasten off and leave a long tail for sewing. Place the hair on the head, secure it with pins, and sew it into place.

Make your own

JACKIE ROBINSON

American baseball player Jackie Robinson fought for equal rights all his life; he was a pioneer, a fighter, and an amazing athlete. Robinson was the first player to break Major League Baseball's color barrier, ending the segregation that had been present in MLB for more than fifty years. Robinson played for the Brooklyn Dodgers and won the Rookie of the Year Award in 1947, establishing himself as one of the best players in the league. Later he was inducted into the Baseball Hall of Fame. They say that behind every successful man there is a woman, and, in Robinson's case, this woman was Rachel Isum, who became his wife in 1946. She and their three children provided Jackie with the emotional support he needed during his fight for equal rights.

MATERIALS

B-1 or C-2 (2.5 mm) crochet hook

⁵⁄₁₆" (8 mm) safety eyes

Tapestry needle

Polyester fiberfill

Black thread for embroidery

Small amount of white felt

YARNS

Scheepjes Catona 100% cotton yarn:

507 Chocolate—skin, 20 g

106 Snow White—shirt, shorts, 20 g

247 Bluebird—hat, undershirt, 18 g

110 Jet Black—hair, shoes, 18 g

074 Mercury—socks, 12 g

115 Hot Red—jersey number, 1 g

HEAD

Start with the skin color.

Rnd 1. 6 sc into magic ring (6).

Rnd 2. 2 sc into each (12).

Rnd 3. {sc, inc} 6 times (18).

Rnd 4. {sc into 2, inc} 6 times (24).

Rnd 5. {sc into 3, inc} 6 times (30).

Rnd 6. {sc into 4, inc} 6 times (36).

Rnd 7. {sc into 5, inc} 6 times (42).

Rnd 8. {sc into 6, inc} 6 times (48).

Rnd 9. {sc into 7, inc} 6 times (54).

Rnds 10–16. Sc into each (54).

Rnd 17. {sc into 8, inc} 6 times (60).

Rnds 18–20. Sc into each (60).

Rnd 21. {sc into 8, dec} 6 times (54).

Rnd 22. {sc into 7, dec} 6 times (48).

Rnd 23. {sc into 6, dec} 6 times (42).

Rnd 24. {sc into 5, dec} 6 times (36).

Add the eyes (see page 126 for guidance).

Rnd 25. {sc into 4, dec} 6 times (30).

Rnd 26. {sc into 3, dec} 6 times (24).

Start to stuff the head.

Rnd 27. {sc into 2, dec} 6 times (18).

Rnd 28. {sc, dec} 6 times (12).

Continue to stuff the head firmly.

Rnd 29. Sc into each FLO (12).

Change to the white shirt yarn.

BODY

Rnd 1. {sc, inc} 6 times (18).

Rnd 2. {sc into 2, inc} 6 times (24).

Rnd 3. Sc into each (24).

Rnd 4. {sc into 3, inc} 6 times (30).

Rnd 5. Sc into each (30).

Rnds 6. {sc into 4, inc} 6 times (36).

Rnds 7–8. Sc into each (36).

Rnd 9. Sc into each (36).

Change to the color of the socks.

Rnd 10. Sc into each BLO (36).

Rnds 11–12. Sc into each (36).

Rnd 13. {sc into 16, dec} 2 times (34).

Rnds 14–15. Sc into each (34).

Do not fasten off, continue with the legs. Stuff the neck and body continuously.

LEGS

To make the legs, divide the work: 14 stitches for each of the legs, and 3 stitches between the legs, both front and back. Mark the stitches with yarn or a stitch marker. Make sure the legs line up with the eyes. If the last stitch of the body is within the 14 stitches for the legs, then continue crocheting. If it is within the 3 stitches, then fasten off, leave a tail for sewing later, and rejoin the sock-colored yarn with a sl st at the back of the doll.

Rnds 1–3. Sc into each (14).

Rnd 4. {sc into 5, dec} 2 times (12).

Rnds 5–8. Sc into each (12).

Stuff the body firmly and stuff the leg as you crochet it.

Rnd 9. {sc into 4, dec} 2 times (10).

Rnds 10–12. Sc into each (10).

Stuff the leg firmly.

Rnd 13. Dec 5 times (5).

Fasten off, sew up the small hole, and weave in the ends. For the second leg, rejoin with a sl st at the back of the doll and work the leg. When finished, sew up the hole between the legs. Weave in the ends.

EYEBROWS AND NOSE

Using black thread, embroider the eyebrows between rounds 12 and 14. With skin-colored yarn, embroider the nose between rounds 18 and 19.

SHORTS

Using the color of the shorts, join with a sl st to a front loop of round 9 at the center back of the body. Work continuously but join with a sl st at the end of each round. Ch 1 at the beginning does not count as sc.

Rnd 1. Ch 1, {sc, inc} 18 times. (54).

Rnds 2–4. Ch 1, sc into each. (54).

Rnd 5. Ch 1, {sc into 4, dec} 9 times. (45).

Rnds 6–8. Ch 1, sc into each. (45).

Rnd 9. Ch 1, dec, sc into each. (44).

Do not fasten off. Divide the piece into two sections of 22 stitches to form the legs of the shorts. Make sure to align the middle of the shorts with the doll's legs, nose, and eyes. Now work each shorts leg continuously but without joining each round with a sl st.

SHORTS LEGS

Rnd 1. Sc into each (22).

Rnd 2. {sc into 5, dec} 3 times, sc into last (19).

Rnd 3. Sc into each (19).

Rnd 4. Sl st into each (19).

Fasten off and weave in the ends. Rejoin to the shorts at the back of the doll for the other shorts leg and repeat rounds 1–4. Fasten off and weave in the ends.

ARMS

Start with the skin color, make two.

Rnd 1. 6 sc into magic ring (6).

Rnd 2. {sc, inc} 3 times (9).

Rnd 3. Sc into each (9).

Rnd 4. {sc into 2, dec} 2 times, sc into last (7).

Rnd 5. Sc into each (7).

Change to the blue undershirt yarn.

Rnds 6–13. Sc into each.

Fasten off and sew the hole closed. Weave in the ends.

SHIRT SLEEVES

Use the white shirt yarn, make two.

Rnd 1. 6 sc into magic ring (6).

Rnd 2. {sc, inc} 3 times (9).

Rnds 3–5. Sc into each (9).

Fasten off and leave a long tail for sewing. Place the arms into the sleeves. Using small stitches, sew the sleeves onto the arms. Sew the sleeved arms onto the body.

SHOES

Use the color of the shoes, make two.

Rnd 1. Ch 4, 2 sc into 2nd ch from hook, sc, 3 sc into next. Continue working on the other side of the foundation chain: sc, 2 sc into last (9).

Rnd 2. Inc 2 times, sc, inc 3 times, sc, inc 2 times (16).

Rnd 3. Sc into each BLO (16).

Rnd 4. Sc into 5, dec 3 times, sc into 5 (13).

Rnd 5. Sc into 6, dec, sc into 5 (12).

Fasten off and leave a long tail for sewing. Add stuffing to the toe of the shoes, position them on the legs, and sew them into place. Weave in the ends.

HAIR

Use the hair color.

Rnd 1. 6 sc into magic ring (6).

Rnd 2. 2 sc into each (12).

Rnd 3. {sc, inc} 6 times (18).

Rnd 4. {sc into 2, inc} 6 times (24).
Rnd 5. {sc into 3, inc} 6 times (30).
Rnd 6. {sc into 4, inc} 6 times (36).
Rnd 7. {sc into 5, inc} 6 times (42).
Rnd 8. {sc into 6, inc} 6 times (48).
Rnd 9. {sc into 7, inc} 6 times (54).
Rnds 10–17. Sc into each (54).
Rnd 18. Sc into 16, hdc into next 4, sl st into next 2, hdc into next 2, dc into next 6, hdc into next 2, sl st into next 2, hdc into next 4, sc into next 16.
Rnd 19. Sc into 6, sl st into next.
Fasten off and leave a long tail for sewing. Place the hair on the head, secure it with pins, and sew it into place.

HAT

Use the color of the hat.
Work each sc in an "X" shape (see page 122) until the hat is complete, or use standard sc if you prefer.
Rnd 1. 6 sc into magic ring (6).
Rnd 2. 2 sc into each (12).
Rnd 3. {sc, inc} 6 times (18).
Rnd 4. {sc into 2, inc} 6 times (24).
Rnd 5. {sc into 3, inc} 6 times (30).
Rnd 6. {sc into 4, inc} 6 times (36).
Rnd 7. {sc into 5, inc} 6 times (42).
Rnd 8. {sc into 6, inc} 6 times (48).
Rnd 9. {sc into 7, inc} 6 times (54).
Rnd 10. {sc into 8, inc} 6 times (60).
Rnds 11–19. Sc into each (60).
Continue crocheting the brim. Work in rows, turning at the end of each row. Ch 1 at the beginning does not count as sc.
Row 20. Ch 1, FLO {sc into 2, inc} 6 times, turn (24).
Row 21. Ch 1, sk first stitch, sc into next 21, dec, turn (22).
Row 22. Ch 1, sk first stitch, sc into next 19, dec, turn (20).

Row 23. Ch 1, sk first stitch, sc into next 17, dec, turn (18).
Row 24. Ch 1, sk first stitch, sc into next 15, dec (16). Do not fasten off, crochet around the hat. Sc into the same stitch, then crochet evenly along the side of the brim (about 4 sc), then sc into each st around the hat, crochet 4 sc along the other side of the brim, and join with a sl st to the first sc of row 24. Fasten off and weave in the ends.

CLOTHING EMBROIDERY

Using white yarn, embroider a letter "B" on the center front of the hat between rounds 13 and 18. Use pins as a guide to help you form the letter. Then, insert the needle behind each white stitch all the way around to produce a thicker white line. Last, embroider the line across the middle of the letter.

Using red yarn, embroider the number 42 onto the left side of the shirt between rounds 6 and 9 of the body.

Make your own

JANE GOODALL

Jane Goodall is an English anthropologist and primatologist. She is best known for studying the social and family life of chimpanzees. By immersing herself in the habitat of the chimps, she developed a close bond with them. She also gave them names instead of numbers, which was not common practice at the time. During her most famous study of chimpanzees—in Gombe, Tanzania, in the 1960s— Jane discovered that chimps experience emotions like joy and sorrow, and that they form long-term bonds. She also discovered that they make and use tools—a groundbreaking discovery. Jane was just twenty-six years old at that time, and she has subsequently spent more than sixty years protecting chimpanzees and their habitats.

MATERIALS

B-1 or C-2 (2.5 mm) crochet hook

5⁄16" (8 mm) safety eyes

Tapestry needle

Polyester fiberfill

Black thread for embroidery

Small amount of white felt

YARNS

Scheepjes Catona 100% cotton yarn:

130 Old Lace—skin, 20 g

502 Camel—shirt, 7 g

506 Caramel—shorts, 7 g

162 Black Coffee—boots, belt, 5 g

522 Primrose—hair, 18 g

HEAD

Start with the skin color.

Rnd 1. 6 sc into magic ring (6).
Rnd 2. 2 sc into each (12).
Rnd 3. {sc, inc} 6 times (18).
Rnd 4. {sc into 2, inc} 6 times (24).
Rnd 5. {sc into 3, inc} 6 times (30).
Rnd 6. {sc into 4, inc} 6 times (36).
Rnd 7. {sc into 5, inc} 6 times (42).
Rnd 8. {sc into 6, inc} 6 times (48).
Rnd 9. {sc into 7, inc} 6 times (54).
Rnds 10–16. Sc into each (54).
Rnd 17. {sc into 8, inc} 6 times (60).
Rnds 18–20. Sc into each (60).
Rnd 21. {sc into 8, dec} 6 times (54).
Rnd 22. {sc into 7, dec} 6 times (48).
Rnd 23. {sc into 6, dec} 6 times (42).
Rnd 24. {sc into 5, dec} 6 times (36).
Add the eyes (see page 126 for guidance).
Rnd 25. {sc into 4, dec} 6 times (30).
Rnd 26. {sc into 3, dec} 6 times (24).
Start to stuff the head.
Rnd 27. {sc into 2, dec} 6 times (18).
Rnd 28. {sc, dec} 6 times (12).
Continue to stuff the head firmly.
Rnd 29. Sc into each FLO (12).
Change to the color of the shirt.

BODY

Rnd 1. {sc, inc} 6 times (18).
Rnd 2. {sc into 2, inc} 6 times (24).
Rnd 3. Sc into each (24).
Rnd 4. {sc into 3, inc} 6 times (30).
Rnd 5. Sc into each (30).
Rnd 6. {sc into 4, inc} 6 times (36).
Rnd 7. Sc into each (36).
Rnd 8. {sc into 5, inc} 6 times (42).
Rnd 9. Sc into each (42).

Rnd 10. Sc into each (42).
Change to the color of the belt.
Rnd 11. Hdc into each (42).
Change to the color of the shorts.
Rnds 12–15. Sc into each (42).
Rnd 16. {sc into 5, dec} 6 times (36).
Rnd 17. {sc into 4, dec} 6 times (30).
Rnd 18. {sc into 3, dec} 6 times (24).
Rnd 19. {sc into 2, dec} 6 times (18).
Stuff the body firmly.
Rnd 20. {sc, dec} 6 times (12).
Rnd 21. Dec 6 times (6).
Fasten off and leave a long tail for sewing. Sew up the hole and weave in the ends.

EYEBROWS AND NOSE

Using black thread, embroider the eyebrows between rounds 12 and 14. With skin-colored yarn, embroider the nose between rounds 18 and 19. You can add a cheek blush with makeup or watercolor pencil.

CLOTHING EMBROIDERY

Using the color of the shorts, embroider the collar and a straight line onto the shirt. Start by pulling the needle through between round 29 of the head and round 1 of the body. Embroider a straight line by pushing the needle into the body right above the belt. Make sure the line aligns with the nose. Pull the needle through between rounds 2 and 3 of the body, two stitches away from the line you just embroidered. Push the needle into the starting point and pull through at the center back of the doll. Finish one side of the collar by pushing the needle into the same stitch where you pulled through between rounds 2 and 3. Pull through between the same rounds on the other side of the line, two stitches away. Finish the other side of the collar in the same way. Weave in the ends. Using the skin-colored yarn, embroider a rectangle onto the belt. Fasten off and weave in the ends.

HAIR

Use the hair color.

Rnd 1. 6 sc into magic ring (6).

Rnd 2. 2 sc into each (12).

Rnd 3. {sc, inc} 6 times (18).

Rnd 4. {sc into 2, inc} 6 times (24).

Rnd 5. {sc into 3, inc} 6 times (30).

Rnd 6. {sc into 4, inc} 6 times (36).

Rnd 7. {sc into 5, inc} 6 times (42).

Rnd 8. {sc into 6, inc} 6 times (48).

Rnd 9. {sc into 7, inc} 6 times (54).

Rnds 10–17. Sc into each (54).

Rnd 18. Dc into next 25, hdc into next, sl st into next 2, hdc into next, dc into last 25 (54).

Fasten off and leave a long tail for sewing.

PONYTAIL

Using the hair color, ch 20, sl st into 2nd ch from hook and into each ch. Join this strand to the hair with a sl st between rounds 13 and 14, right above where you fastened off the hair. ★ Ch 20, sl st into 2nd ch from hook and into each ch. Join to the hair with a sl st next to the previous strand. Repeat from ★ 4 times. Fasten off and weave in the ends. Place the hair on the head, secure it with pins, and sew it into place. Using the color of the shorts, wind some yarn around the ponytail a few times, close to the hair. Weave in the ends.

ARMS

Use the skin color, make two.

Rnd 1. 6 sc into magic ring (6).

Rnd 2. {sc, inc} 3 times (9).

Rnd 3. Sc into each (9).

Rnd 4. {sc into 2, dec} 2 times, sc into last (7).

Rnds 5–13. Sc into each (7).

Fasten off and sew the hole closed. Weave in the ends.

SHIRT SLEEVES

Use the color of the shirt, make two.

Rnd 1. 6 sc into magic ring (6).

Rnd 2. {sc, inc} 3 times (9).

Rnds 3–5. Sc into each (9).

Fasten off and leave a long tail for sewing. Place the arms into the sleeves. Using small stitches, sew the sleeves onto the arms. Sew the sleeved arms onto the body.

LEGS

Start with the skin color, make two.

Rnd 1. 6 sc into magic ring (6).

Rnd 2. {sc, inc} 3 times (9).

Rnd 3. {sc into 2, inc} 3 times (12).

Rnds 4–10. Sc into each (12).

Change to the color of the boots.

Rnd 11. Sc into each (12).

Rnd 12. Inc 2 times, sc into 10 (14).

Rnd 13. Inc 4 times, sc into 10 (18).

Rnds 14–15. Sc into each (18).

Rnd 16. BLO dec 9 times (9).

Stuff the leg firmly.

Rnd 17. Dec 3 more times.

Stuff the toe of each leg. Fasten off and leave a long tail for sewing. Sew up the hole and weave in the ends.

SHORTS LEGS

Use the color of the shorts, make two.

Rnd 1. 6 sc into magic ring (6).

Rnd 2. Inc 6 times (12).

Rnd 3. {sc into 2, inc} 4 times (16).

Rnds 4–6. Sc into each (16).

Rnd 7. Sc into 3, sl st into 13 (16).

Rnd 8. Sl st into first 3.

Fasten off and leave a long tail for sewing. Place the legs into the shorts legs and sew the shorts onto the legs. Sew the finished legs onto the body continuously from the shorts legs to the boots.

Make your own

MALALA YOUSAFZAI

Malala Yousafzai is a Pakistan-born activist and human rights advocate. She was just eleven years old when the Taliban took control of the town where she lived and banned girls from attending school. She spoke out about girls' rights to an education and became recognized for her activism. In 2012, a Taliban gunman shot her as she rode home on a bus. She woke up ten days later in a hospital in the UK. After several months of rehabilitation, she recovered and continued to fight for education and equality for girls. She founded the nonprofit organization Malala Fund with her father to fight for every girl's right to an education. At the age of seventeen, she was the corecipient of the 2014 Nobel Peace Prize for her work, and she became the youngest Nobel laureate.

MATERIALS

B-1 or C-2 (2.5 mm) crochet hook

5/16" (8 mm) safety eyes

Tapestry needle

Polyester fiberfill

Black thread for embroidery

Small amount of white felt

YARNS

Scheepjes Catona 100% cotton yarn:

502 Camel—skin, 20 g

391 Deep Ocean Green—shirt, 8 g

074 Mercury—pants, 10 g

162 Black Coffee—shoes, 3 g

110 Jet Black—hair, 18 g

517 Ruby—headscarf, 22 g

383 Ginger Gold—headscarf, 4 g

408 Old Rose—embroidery, 1 g

403 Lemonade—embroidery, 1 g

HEAD

Start with the skin color.

Rnd 1. 6 sc into magic ring (6).

Rnd 2. 2 sc into each (12).

Rnd 3. {sc, inc} 6 times (18).

Rnd 4. {sc into 2, inc} 6 times (24).

Rnd 5. {sc into 3, inc} 6 times (30).

Rnd 6. {sc into 4, inc} 6 times (36).

Rnd 7. {sc into 5, inc} 6 times (42).

Rnd 8. {sc into 6, inc} 6 times (48).

Rnd 9. {sc into 7, inc} 6 times (54).

Rnds 10–16. Sc into each (54).

Rnd 17. {sc into 8, inc} 6 times (60).

Rnds 18–20. Sc into each (60).

Rnd 21. {sc into 8, dec} 6 times (54).

Rnd 22. {sc into 7, dec} 6 times (48).

Rnd 23. {sc into 6, dec} 6 times (42).

Rnd 24. {sc into 5, dec} 6 times (36).

Add the eyes (see page 126 for guidance).

Rnd 25. {sc into 4, dec} 6 times (30).

Rnd 26. {sc into 3, dec} 6 times (24).

Start to stuff the head.

Rnd 27. {sc into 2, dec} 6 times (18).

Rnd 28. {sc, dec} 6 times (12).

Continue to stuff the head firmly.

Rnd 29. Sc into each FLO (12).

Change to the color of the shirt.

BODY

Rnd 1. {sc, inc} 6 times (18).

Rnd 2. {sc into 2, inc} 6 times (24).

Rnd 3. Sc into each (24).

Rnd 4. {sc into 3, inc} 6 times (30).

Rnd 5. Sc into each (30).

Rnd 6. {sc into 4, inc} 6 times (36).

Rnds 7–9. Sc into each (36).

Rnd 10. Sc into each BLO (36).

Change to the color of the pants.

Rnds 11–12. Sc into each (36).

Rnd 13. {sc into 16, dec} 2 times (34).

Rnds 14–15. Sc into each (34).

Do not fasten off, continue with the legs. Stuff the neck and body continuously.

LEGS

To make the legs, divide the work: 14 stitches for each of the legs, and 3 stitches between the legs, both front and back. Mark the stitches with yarn or a stitch marker. Make sure the legs line up with the eyes. If the last stitch of the body is within the 14 stitches for the legs, then continue crocheting. If it is within the 3 stitches, then fasten off, leave a tail for sewing later, and rejoin the pants-colored yarn with a sl st at the back of the doll.

Rnds 1–3. Sc into each (14).

Rnd 4. {sc into 5, dec} 2 times (12).

Rnds 5–8. Sc into each (12).

Stuff the body firmly and stuff the leg as you crochet it.

Rnd 9. {sc into 4, dec} 2 times (10).

Change to the skin color.

Rnd 10. Sc into each BLO (10).

Rnds 11–12. Sc into each (10).

Stuff the leg firmly.

Rnd 13. Dec 5 times (5).

Fasten off, sew up the small hole, and weave in the ends. With the color of the pants, crochet sl sts into each front loop of round 9. For the second leg, rejoin with a sl st at the back of the doll and work the leg. When finished, sew up the hole between the legs. Weave in the ends.

FINISHING THE SHIRT

Using the color of the shirt, join with a sl st to a front loop of round 9 at the center back of the body. Work continuously, but join with a sl st at the end of each round. Ch 1 at the beginning does not count as sc.

Rnds 1–5. Ch 1, sc into each (36).

Rnd 6. Ch 1, sl st into each (36).
Fasten off and weave in the ends.

SHIRT EMBROIDERY

The first row of the embroidery is on round 3 of the
body. Using the pink yarn, pull the needle through
between rounds 3 and 4, and embroider a "V" shape.
Skip four stitches and pull the needle through again.
Repeat, embroidering "V" shapes until you are four
stitches away from the first one. Continue embroidering
in the same way between rounds 4 and 6, 6 and 8, 8 and
10, and 11 and 13. Use the yellow yarn to embroider a
line into the middle of each "V" shape. Weave in the ends.

EYEBROWS AND NOSE

Using black thread, embroider the eyebrows between
rounds 12 and 14. With skin-colored yarn, embroider
the nose between rounds 18 and 19.

SHOES

Use the color of the shoes, make two.
Rnd 1. Ch 4, 2 sc into 2nd ch from hook, sc, 3 sc
into next. Continue working on the other side of the
foundation chain: sc, 2 sc into last (9).
Rnd 2. Inc 2 times, sc, inc 3 times, sc, inc 2 times (16).
Rnd 3. Sc into each BLO (16).
Rnd 4. Sc into 5, dec 3 times, sc into 5 (13).
Rnd 5. Sc into 5, dec, sc into 6 (12).
Fasten off and leave a long tail for sewing. Add stuffing
to the toe of the shoes, position them on the legs, and
sew them into place. Weave in the ends.

ARMS

Start with the skin color, make two.
Rnd 1. 6 sc into magic ring (6).
Rnd 2. {sc, inc} 3 times (9).
Rnd 3. Sc into each (9).
Rnd 4. {sc, dec} 3 times (6).
Rnds 5–7. Sc into each (6).
Change to the color of the shirt.
Rnds 8–12. Sc into each (6).
Fasten off and leave a long tail for sewing. Position an
arm on each side of the doll and sew them into place.

HAIR

Use the hair color.
Rnd 1. 6 sc into magic ring (6).
Rnd 2. 2 sc into each (12).
Rnd 3. {sc, inc} 6 times (18).
Rnd 4. {sc into 2, inc} 6 times (24).
Rnd 5. {sc into 3, inc} 6 times (30).
Rnd 6. {sc into 4, inc} 6 times (36).

Rnd 7. {sc into 5, inc} 6 times (42).

Rnd 8. {sc into 6, inc} 6 times (48).

Rnd 9. {sc into 7, inc} 6 times (54).

Rnds 10–17. Sc into each (54).

Rnd 18. Sc into next, sl st into next 2, hdc into next 2, dc into next 47, hdc into next 2 (54).

Fasten off and leave a long tail for sewing.

PONYTAIL

Using the hair color, ch 22, sl st into 2nd ch from hook and into each ch. Join this strand to the back of the hair with a sl st between rounds 15 and 16. ★ Ch 22, sl st into 2nd ch from hook and into each ch. Join to the hair with a sl st next to the previous strand. Repeat from ★ 4 times. Fasten off and leave a long tail. Wrap yarn around the ponytail a few times close to the hair. Weave in the ends. Place the hair on the head, secure it with pins, and sew it into place.

HEADSCARF

Start with the pink headscarf yarn. Work in rows, turning at the end of each row. Ch 2 at the beginning does not count as hdc.

Row 1. Ch 7, hdc into 2nd ch from hook and into next 4 (5).

Rows 2–12. Ch 2, hdc into each (5).

Row 13. Ch 2, {hdc, inc} 2 times, hdc into last (7).

Rows 14–17. Ch 2, hdc into each (7).

Row 18. Ch 2, {hdc, inc} 3 times, hdc into last (10).

Rows 19–21. Ch 2, hdc into each (10).

Row 22. Ch 2, {hdc, inc} 5 times (15).

Row 23. Ch 2, hdc into each (15).

Row 24. Ch 2, {hdc, inc} 3 times, hdc into 9 (18).

Row 25. Ch 2, hdc into each (18).

Row 26. Ch 2, {hdc into 2, inc} 3 times, hdc into 9 (21).

Rows 27–29. Ch 2, hdc into each (21).

Row 30. Ch 2, {hdc, inc} 3 times, hdc into 15 (24).

Rows 31–35. Ch 2, hdc into each (24).

Row 36. Ch 2, {hdc, dec} 3 times, hdc into 15 (21).

Rows 37–39. Ch 2, hdc into each (21).

Row 40. Ch 2, {hdc into 2, dec} 3 times, hdc into 9 (18).

Row 41. Ch 2, hdc into each (18).

Row 42. Ch 2, {hdc, dec} 3 times, hdc into 9 (15).

Row 43. Ch 2, hdc into each (15).

Row 44. Ch 2, {hdc, dec} 5 times (10).

Rows 45–47. Ch 2, hdc into each (10).

Row 48. Ch 2, {hdc, dec} 3 times, hdc into last (7).

Rows 49–53. Ch 2, hdc into each (7).

Row 54. Ch 2, {hdc, dec} 2 times, hdc into last (5).

Rows 55–66. Ch 2, hdc into each (5).

Change to the yellow headscarf yarn. Without turning the piece, start crocheting evenly along the straight edge of the scarf (working toward the left). Crochet 24 sc evenly on 24 rows of the scarf (if you place the scarf in front of you, there are two rows between two horizontal lines). Dec 10 times on 20 rows of the scarf, then crochet 24 sc evenly on 24 rows of the scarf. This will be the bottom edge of the scarf. Continue crocheting sc evenly on the side, front, and the other side. Join with a sl st into the first sc. Fasten off and weave in the ends.

Make your own

AUDREY HEPBURN

It's almost impossible not to admire the British actress and humanitarian Audrey Hepburn. She was one of the most successful actresses of the Golden Age of Hollywood, winning an Oscar for her very first starring role in *Roman Holiday,* and following it up with amazing performances in films such as *Sabrina*, *Breakfast at Tiffany's*, and *My Fair Lady.* She was and still is a style icon—she was the muse of Givenchy—and her signature looks, the black turtleneck, black trousers, ballet flats, and the little black dress, are still so stylish today. In later life she became a goodwill ambassador for UNICEF and devoted her time to humanitarian projects.

MATERIALS

B-1 or C-2 (2.5 mm) crochet hook

5/16" (8 mm) safety eyes

Tapestry needle

Polyester fiberfill

Black thread for embroidery

5/8 x 16" (1.5 x 40 cm) satin ribbon

Small amount of white felt

YARNS

Scheepjes Catona 100% cotton yarn:

130 Old Lace—skin, 25 g

110 Jet Black—dress, hat, shoes, 25 g

162 Black Coffee—hair, 20 g

HEAD

Start with the skin color.

Rnd 1. 6 sc into magic ring (6).

Rnd 2. 2 sc into each (12).

Rnd 3. {sc, inc} 6 times (18).

Rnd 4. {sc into 2, inc} 6 times (24).

Rnd 5. {sc into 3, inc} 6 times (30).

Rnd 6. {sc into 4, inc} 6 times (36).

Rnd 7. {sc into 5, inc} 6 times (42).

Rnd 8. {sc into 6, inc} 6 times (48).

Rnd 9. {sc into 7, inc} 6 times (54).

Rnds 10–16. Sc into each (54).

Rnd 17. {sc into 8, inc} 6 times (60).

Rnds 18–20. Sc into each (60).

Rnd 21. {sc into 8, dec} 6 times (54).

Rnd 22. {sc into 7, dec} 6 times (48).

Rnd 23. {sc into 6, dec} 6 times (42).

Rnd 24. {sc into 5, dec} 6 times (36).

Add the eyes (see page 126 for guidance).

Rnd 25. {sc into 4, dec} 6 times (30).

Rnd 26. {sc into 3, dec} 6 times (24).

Start to stuff the head.

Rnd 27. {sc into 2, dec} 6 times (18).

Rnd 28. {sc, dec} 6 times (12).

Continue to stuff the head firmly.

Rnd 29. Sc into each FLO (12).

Do not fasten off, continue with the body.

BODY

Rnd 1. {sc, inc} 6 times (18).

Change to the color of the dress. Work each sc in an "X" shape (see page 122) until the the change to skin color.

Rnd 2. {sc into 2, inc} 6 times (24).

Rnd 3. Sc into each (24).

Rnd 4. {sc into 3, inc} 6 times (30).

Rnd 5. Sc into each (30).

Rnd 6. {sc into 4, inc} 6 times (36).

Rnds 7–8. Sc into each (36).

Rnd 9. Sc into each (36).

Change to the skin color.

Rnd 10. Sc into each BLO (36).

Rnds 11–12. Sc into each (36).

Rnd 13. {sc into 16, dec} 2 times (34).

Rnds 14–15. Sc into each (34).

Do not fasten off, continue with the legs. Stuff the neck and body continuously.

LEGS

To make the legs, divide the work: 14 stitches for each of the legs, and 3 stitches between the legs, both front and back. Mark the stitches with yarn or a stitch marker. Make sure the legs line up with the eyes. If the last stitch of the body is within the 14 stitches for the legs, then continue crocheting. If it is within the 3 stitches, then fasten off, leave a tail for sewing later, and rejoin the skin-colored yarn with a sl st at the back of the doll.

Rnds 1–3. Sc into each (14).

Rnd 4. {sc into 5, dec} 2 times (12).

Rnds 5–8. Sc into each (12).

Stuff the body firmly and stuff the leg as you crochet it.

Rnd 9. {sc into 4, dec} 2 times (10).

Rnds 10–12. Sc into each (10).

Stuff the leg firmly.

Rnd 13. Dec 5 times (5).

Fasten off, sew up the small hole, and weave in the ends. For the second leg, rejoin with a sl st at the back of the doll and work the leg. When finished, sew up the hole between the legs. Weave in the ends.

SKIRT

Using the color of the dress, join with a sl st to a front loop of round 9 at the center back of the body. Work continuously but join with a sl st at the end of each round. Ch 1 at the beginning does not count as sc. Work each sc in an "X" shape (see page 122) until the skirt is complete.

Rnd 1. Ch 1, 2 sc into each (72).

Rnds 2–3. Ch 1, sc into each (72).

Rnd 4. Ch 1, {sc into 4, dec} 12 times (60).

Rnds 5–13. Ch 1, sc into each (60).

Rnd 14. Sl st into each (60).

Fasten off and weave in the ends.

EYEBROWS AND NOSE

Using black thread, embroider the eyebrows between rounds 12 and 14. With skin-colored yarn, embroider the nose between rounds 18 and 19. You can add a cheek blush with makeup or watercolor pencil.

ARMS

Use the skin color, make two.

Rnd 1. 6 sc into magic ring (6).

Rnd 2. {sc, inc} 3 times (9).

Rnd 3. Sc into each (9).

Rnd 4. {sc into 3, dec} 3 times (6).

Rnds 5–11. Sc into each (6).

Fasten off and sew the hole closed. Weave in the ends.

DRESS SLEEVES

Use the color of the dress, make two.

Rnd 1. 6 sc into magic ring (6).

Rnd 2. {sc, inc} 3 times (9).

Rnd 3. Sc into each (9).

Fasten off and leave a long tail for sewing. Place the arms into the sleeves. Using small stitches, sew the sleeves onto the arms. Sew the sleeved arms onto the body.

SHOES

Use the color of the shoes, make two.

Rnd 1. 6 sc into magic ring (6).

Rnd 2. {sc, inc} 3 times (9).

Rnd 3. {sc into 2, inc} 3 times (12).

Rnd 4. Sc into each (12).

Fasten off and leave a long tail for sewing. Position them on the legs and sew them into place. Weave in the ends.

HAIR

Use the hair color.

Rnd 1. 6 sc into magic ring (6).

Rnd 2. 2 sc into each (12).

Rnd 3. {sc, inc} 6 times (18).

Rnd 4. {sc into 2, inc} 6 times (24).

Rnd 5. {sc into 3, inc} 6 times (30).

Rnd 6. {sc into 4, inc} 6 times (36).

Rnd 7. {sc into 5, inc} 6 times (42).

Rnd 8. {sc into 6, inc} 6 times (48).

Rnd 9. {sc into 7, inc} 6 times (54).

Rnds 10–17. Sc into each (54).

Rnd 18. Sl st into next, ★ ch 6, sl st into 2nd ch from hook and next 4, sl st into next on the wig. Repeat from ★ 3 times. ★★ Ch 5, sl st into 2nd ch from hook and next 3, sl st into next on the wig. Repeat from ★★ 2 times. ★★★ Ch 3, sl st into 2nd ch from hook and next, sl st into next on the wig. Repeat from ★★★ once more. Sc into next 42, sl st into last.

Fasten off and leave a long tail for sewing. Place the hair on the head, secure it with pins, and sew it into place.

BUN

Use the hair color.

Rnd 1. 6 sc into magic ring (6).

Rnd 2. 2 sc into each (12

Rnd 3. {sc, inc} 6 times (18).

Rnd 4. {sc into 2, inc} 6 times (24).

Rnd 5. {sc into 3, inc} 6 times (30).

Rnd 6. {sc into 4, inc} 6 times (36).

Rnds 7–8. Sc into each (36).

Rnd 9. {sc into 4, dec} 6 times (30).

Fasten off and leave a long tail for sewing. Place the bun on the head between rounds 9 and 18 of the hair. Secure the bun with pins, stuff it, and sew it into place.

HAT

Use the color of the hat.

Rnd 1. 7 sc into magic ring (7).

Rnd 2. 2 sc into each (14).

Rnd 3. {sc, inc} 7 times (21).

Rnd 4. {sc into 2, inc} 7 times (28).

Rnd 5. {sc into 3, inc} 7 times (35).

Rnd 6. {sc into 4, inc} 7 times (42).

Rnd 7. {sc into 5, inc} 7 times (49).

Rnd 8. {sc into 6, inc} 7 times (56).

Rnds 9–11. Sc into each (56).

Rnd 12. Hdc into each FLO of round 11 (56).

Rnd 13. Sc into each BLO of round 11 (56).

Rnd 14. {sc into 7, inc} 7 times (63).

Rnd 15. Sc into each (63).

Rnd 16. {sc into 8, inc} 7 times (70).

Rnds 17–18. Sc into each (70).

Rnd 19. Sl st into each (70).

Fasten off and weave in the ends. Using black thread, sew the center of the satin ribbon onto the back of the hat where you fastened off. Twist the ribbon and sew it onto the hat 1¾" (4.5 cm) from where you first stitched it. Twist the ribbon again and sew it onto the hat 1¾" (4.5 cm) from the previous sewn point. Repeat this twist and sew method on the other side of the hat. Tie a knot with the rest of the ribbon and trim the ends.

Make your own

SERENA WILLIAMS

Serena Williams is undoubtedly the greatest female tennis player of all time. The American athlete has won twenty-three Grand Slam singles titles—the most of any player in the Open Era of tennis—but she is so much more than just an athlete. Serena Williams is an example of how to make a difference. She is a fighter on and off the court, who tries to change the system and fights for women's rights in sports. She gave birth to her first child in 2017 and was eight weeks pregnant when she won the Australian Open. She is a champion on and off the court—a real icon.

MATERIALS

B-1 or C-2 (2.5 mm) crochet hook

5⁄16" (8 mm) safety eyes

Tapestry needle

Polyester fiberfill

Black thread for embroidery

Small amount of white felt

YARNS

Scheepjes Catona 100% cotton yarn:

507 Chocolate—skin, 20 g

258 Rosewood—dress, headband, 15 g

252 Watermelon—shoes (A), 2 g

110 Jet Black—belt, shoes (B), 3 g

106 Snow White—shoes (C), 1 g

162 Black Coffee—hair, 18 g

502 Camel—curls, 8 g

HEAD

Start with the skin color.

Rnd 1. 6 sc into magic ring (6).

Rnd 2. 2 sc into each (12).

Rnd 3. {sc, inc} 6 times (18).

Rnd 4. {sc into 2, inc} 6 times (24).

Rnd 5. {sc into 3, inc} 6 times (30).

Rnd 6. {sc into 4, inc} 6 times (36).

Rnd 7. {sc into 5, inc} 6 times (42).

Rnd 8. {sc into 6, inc} 6 times (48).

Rnd 9. {sc into 7, inc} 6 times (54).

Rnds 10–16. Sc into each (54).

Rnd 17. {sc into 8, inc} 6 times (60).

Rnds 18–20. Sc into each (60).

Rnd 21. {sc into 8, dec} 6 times (54).

Rnd 22. {sc into 7, dec} 6 times (48).

Rnd 23. {sc into 6, dec} 6 times (42).

Rnd 24. {sc into 5, dec} 6 times (36).

Add the eyes (see page 126 for guidance).

Rnd 25. {sc into 4, dec} 6 times (30).

Rnd 26. {sc into 3, dec} 6 times (24).

Start to stuff the head.

Rnd 27. {sc into 2, dec} 6 times (18).

Rnd 28. {sc, dec} 6 times (12).

Continue to stuff the head firmly.

Rnd 29. Sc into each FLO (12).

Change to the color of the dress.

BODY

Rnd 1. {sc, inc} 6 times (18).

Rnd 2. {sc into 2, inc} 6 times (24).

Rnd 3. Sc into each (24).

Rnd 4. {sc into 3, inc} 6 times (30).

Rnd 5. Sc into each (30).

Rnd 6. {sc into 4, inc} 6 times (36).

Rnd 7. Sc into each (36).

Rnd 8. Sc into each (36).

Change to the color of the belt.

Rnd 9. Sc into each (36).

Change to the color of the dress.

Rnd 10. Sc into each BLO (36).

Rnds 11–12. Sc into each (36).

Rnd 13. {sc into 16, dec} 2 times (34).

Rnds 14–15. Sc into each (34).

Fasten off and weave in the ends. Stuff the neck and body continuously.

LEGS

To make the legs, divide the work: 14 stitches for each of the legs, and 3 stitches between the legs, both front and back. Mark the stitches with yarn or a stitch marker. Make sure the legs line up with the eyes. Use skin-colored yarn and join with a sl st at the back of the doll to start.

Rnds 1–3. Sc into each (14).

Rnd 4. {sc into 5, dec} 2 times (12).

Rnds 5–8. Sc into each (12).

Stuff the body firmly and stuff the leg as you crochet it.

Rnd 9. {sc into 4, dec} 2 times (10).

Rnds 10–12. Sc into each (10).

Stuff the leg firmly.

Rnd 13. Dec 5 times (5).

Fasten off, sew up the small hole, and weave in the ends. For the second leg, rejoin with a sl st at the back of the doll and work the leg. When finished, sew up the hole between the legs. Weave in the ends.

SKIRT

Using the color of the dress, join with a sl st to a front loop of round 9 at the center back of the body. Work continuously but join with a sl st at the end of each round. Ch 2 at the beginning does not count as dc.

Rnd 1. Ch 2, {dc, inc} 18 times (54).

Rnd 2. Ch 2, dc into each (54).

Rnd 3. Ch 2, hdc into each (54).

Rnd 4. Sl st into each (54).

Fasten off and weave in the ends.

Round 1, Skirt

EYEBROWS AND NOSE

Using black thread, embroider the eyebrows between rounds 12 and 14. With skin-colored yarn, embroider the nose between rounds 18 and 19.

ARMS

Start with the skin color, make two.

Rnd 1. 6 sc into magic ring (6).

Rnd 2. {sc, inc} 3 times (9).

Rnd 3. Sc into each (9).

Rnd 4. {sc into 1, dec} 3 times (6).

Change to the color of the dress.

Rnds 5–12. Sc into each (6).

Fasten off and leave a long tail for sewing. Position an arm on each side of the doll and sew them into place.

SHOES

Start with shoe color A, make two.

Rnd 1. Ch 4, 2 sc into 2nd ch from hook, sc, 3 sc into next. Continue working on the other side of the foundation chain: sc, 2 sc into last (9).

Rnd 2. Inc 2 times, sc, inc 3 times, sc, inc 2 times (16). Change to shoe color B.

Rnd 3. Sc into each BLO (16).

Rnd 4. Sc into 5, dec 3 times, sc into 5 (13).

Rnd 5. Sc into 6, dec, sc into 5 (12). Change to shoe color C.

Rnd 6. Sc into each (12).

Fasten off and leave a long tail for sewing. Add stuffing to the toe of the shoes, position them on the legs, and sew them into place. Weave in the ends.

HAIR

Use the dark brown hair color.

Rnd 1. 6 sc into magic ring (6).

Rnd 2. 2 sc into each (12).

Rnd 3. {sc, inc} 6 times (18).

Rnd 4. {sc into 2, inc} 6 times (24).

Rnd 5. {sc into 3, inc} 6 times (30).

Rnd 6. {sc into 4, inc} 6 times (36).

Rnd 7. {sc into 5, inc} 6 times (42).

Rnd 8. {sc into 6, inc} 6 times (48).

Rnd 9. {sc into 7, inc} 6 times (54).

Rnds 10–19. Sc into each (54).

Fasten off and leave a long tail for sewing. Place the hair on the head, secure it with pins, and sew it into place.

BUN

Use the dark brown hair color.

Rnd 1. 6 sc into magic ring (6).

Rnd 2. 2 sc into each (12).

Rnd 3. {sc, inc} 6 times (18).

Rnd 4. {sc into 2, inc} 6 times (24).

Rnd 5. {sc into 3, inc} 6 times (30).

Rnds 6–7. Sc into each (30).

Change to the lighter curls color.

Rnds 8–9. Sc into each (30).

Fasten off and leave a long tail for sewing.

CURLS

Use the color of the curls, make five.
Ch 32, 2 hdc into 3rd ch from hook and next 27,
sc into last 2. Fasten off and leave a long tail for sewing.
Place three of the curls on top of the head at about
round 2 of the hair. Place them as close together as
possible so that the bun will cover the tops of the curls.
Sew the three curls into place. Place the other two curls
on top of the first three and sew them on. Weave in the
ends. Slightly stuff the bun and position it on the head so
that half of the bun covers the tops of the curls and half
lies on the hair. Continue to stuff the bun while you sew
it into place.

HAIRBAND

Use the dress color. Leave a long tail at the beginning,
then ch 28. Fasten off and leave a long tail. Wrap the chain
around the bun and tie a knot below the curls. Weave in
the ends.

HEADBAND

Use the dress color. Leave a long tail at the beginning,
then ch 70. Fasten off and leave a long tail. Wrap the
chain around the head between rounds 13 and 14 and
sew both ends to the hair, next to each other. Weave in
the ends.

Make your own

MUHAMMAD ALI

American Muhammad Ali was one of the most influential athletes in the history of sport. For many, he was and still is the greatest boxer of all time, but he was also an activist who fought for equal rights. Ali was the first fighter to win the world heavyweight championship on three separate occasions, and he defended his title nineteen times. In 1961 he converted to Islam and became a Muslim, which defined not only his life but also his sporting career. He refused to be drafted into the military and fight in Vietnam, and as a result was stripped of his titles and suspended from boxing for four years—but he fought his way back to the top and became champion again.

MATERIALS

B-1 or C-2 (2.5 mm) crochet hook

⁵⁄₁₆" (8 mm) safety eyes

Tapestry needle

Polyester fiberfill

Black thread for embroidery

Small amount of white felt

YARNS

Scheepjes Catona 100% cotton yarn:

507 Chocolate—skin, 25 g

106 Snow White—shorts, shoes, 10 g

110 Jet Black—hair, belt, 18 g

115 Hot Red—boxing gloves, 8 g

HEAD

Start with the skin color.

Rnd 1. 6 sc into magic ring (6).

Rnd 2. 2 sc into each (12).

Rnd 3. {sc, inc} 6 times (18).

Rnd 4. {sc into 2, inc} 6 times (24).

Rnd 5. {sc into 3, inc} 6 times (30).

Rnd 6. {sc into 4, inc} 6 times (36).

Rnd 7. {sc into 5, inc} 6 times (42).

Rnd 8. {sc into 6, inc} 6 times (48).

Rnd 9. {sc into 7, inc} 6 times (54).

Rnds 10–16. Sc into each (54).

Rnd 17. {sc into 8, inc} 6 times (60).

Rnds 18–20. Sc into each (60).

Rnd 21. {sc into 8, dec} 6 times (54).

Rnd 22. {sc into 7, dec} 6 times (48).

Rnd 23. {sc into 6, dec} 6 times (42).

Rnd 24. {sc into 5, dec} 6 times (36).

Add the eyes (see page 126 for guidance).

Rnd 25. {sc into 4, dec} 6 times (30).

Rnd 26. {sc into 3, dec} 6 times (24).

Start to stuff the head.

Rnd 27. {sc into 2, dec} 6 times (18).

Rnd 28. {sc, dec} 6 times (12).

Continue to stuff the head firmly.

Rnd 29. Sc into each FLO (12).

Do not fasten off, continue with the body.

BODY

Rnd 1. {sc, inc} 6 times (18).

Rnd 2. {sc into 2, inc} 6 times (24).

Rnd 3. Sc into each (24).

Rnd 4. {sc into 3, inc} 6 times (30).

Rnd 5. Sc into each (30).

Rnd 6. {sc into 4, inc} 6 times (36).

Rnd 7. Sc into each (36).

Rnd 8. Sc into each (36).

Change to the color of the belt.

Rnd 9. Hdc into each (36). Change to the skin color.

Rnd 10. Sc into each BLO (36).

Rnds 11–12. Sc into each (36).

Rnd 13. {sc into 16, dec} 2 times (34).

Rnd 14. Sc into each (34).

Do not fasten off, continue with the legs. Stuff the neck and body continuously.

LEGS

To make the legs, divide the work: 14 stitches for each of the legs, and 3 stitches between the legs, both front and back. Mark the stitches with yarn or a stitch marker. Make sure the legs line up with the eyes. If the last stitch of the body is within the 14 stitches for the legs, then continue crocheting. If it is within the 3 stitches, then fasten off, leave a tail for sewing later, and rejoin the skin-colored yarn with a sl st at the back of the doll.

Rnds 1–3. Sc into each (14).

Rnd 4. {sc into 5, dec} 2 times (12).

Rnds 5–8. Sc into each (12).

Stuff the body firmly and stuff the leg as you crochet it.

Rnd 9. {sc into 4, dec} 2 times (10).

Rnds 10–12. Sc into each (10).

Stuff the leg firmly.

Rnd 13. Dec 5 times (5).

Fasten off, sew up the small hole, and weave in the ends. For the second leg, rejoin with a sl st at the back of the doll and work the leg. When finished, sew up the hole between the legs. Weave in the ends.

EYEBROWS AND NOSE

Using black thread, embroider the eyebrows between rounds 12 and 14. With skin-colored yarn, embroider the nose between rounds 18 and 19.

SHORTS

Using the color of the shorts, join with a sl st to a front loop of round 9 at the center back of the body. Work continuously but join with a sl st at the end of each round. Ch 1 at the beginning does not count as sc.

Rnd 1. Ch 1, {sc, inc} 18 times. (54).

Rnds 2–4. Ch 1, sc into each. (54).

Rnd 5. Ch 1, {sc into 4, dec} 9 times. (45).

Rnd 6. Ch 1, sc into each. (45).

Rnd 7. Ch 1, dec, sc into each. (44).

Do not fasten off. Divide the piece into two sections of 22 stitches to form the legs of the shorts. Make sure to align the middle of the shorts with the doll's legs, nose, and eyes. Now work each shorts leg continuously, but without joining each round with a sl st.

SHORTS LEGS

Rnd 1. Sc into each (22).

Fasten off and weave in the ends. Rejoin to the shorts at the back of the doll for the other shorts leg and repeat round 1.Fasten off and weave in the ends.

ARMS AND BOXING GLOVES

LEFT

Start with the color of the boxing gloves.

Rnd 1. Ch 3, 2 sc into 2nd ch from hook, 3 sc into next.

Continue on the other side of the foundation chain: sc into last (6).

Rnd 2. {inc, sc into next} 3 times (9).

Rnd 3. {sc into 2, inc} 3 times (12).

Rnds 4–5. Sc into each (12).

Rnd 6. Sc into next, 4 hdc into next and form a popcorn stitch (see page 124), sc into 10 (12).

Rnd 7. {sc into 2, dec} 3 times (9).

Rnd 8. {sc into 2, dec} 2 times, sc into last (7).

Change to the skin color.

Rnds 9–15. Sc into each (7).

Fasten off and leave a long tail for sewing. Using a needle and the red yarn, pull together the palm part of the glove.

RIGHT Start with the color of the boxing gloves.

Rnd 1. Ch 3, 2 sc into 2nd ch from hook, 3 sc into next. Continue on the other side of the foundation chain: sc into last (6).

Rnd 2. {inc, sc into next} 3 times (9).

Rnd 3. {sc into 2, inc} 3 times (12).

Rnds 4–5. Sc into each (12).

Rnd 6. Sc into 6, 4 hdc into next and form a popcorn stitch (see page 124), sc into 5 (12).

Rnd 7. {dec, sc into 2} 3 times (9).

Rnd 8. {sc into 2, dec} 2 times, sc into last (7).

Change to the skin color.

Rnds 9–15. Sc into each (7).

Fasten off and leave a long tail for sewing. Using a needle and the red yarn, pull together the palm part of the glove.

Position an arm on each side of the doll and sew them into place.

SHOES

Use the color of the shoes, make two.

Rnd 1. Ch 4, 2 sc into 2nd ch from hook, sc, 3 sc into next. Continue working on the other side of the foundation chain: sc, 2 sc into last (9).

Rnd 2. Inc 2 times, sc, inc 3 times, sc, inc 2 times (16).

Rnd 3. Sc into each BLO (16).

Rnd 4. Sc into 5, dec 3 times, sc into 5 (13).

Rnd 5. Sc into 6, dec, sc into 5 (12).

Rnds 6–7. Sc into each (12).

Fasten off and leave a long tail for sewing. Add stuffing to the toe of the shoes, position them on the legs, and sew them into place. Weave in the ends.

HAIR

Use the hair color.

Rnd 1. 6 sc into magic ring (6).

Rnd 2. 2 sc in each (12).

Rnd 3. {sc, inc} 6 times (18).

Rnd 4. {sc into 2, inc} 6 times (24).

Rnd 5. {sc into 3, inc} 6 times (30).

Rnd 6. {sc into 4, inc} 6 times (36).

Rnd 7. {sc into 5, inc} 6 times (42).

Rnd 8. {sc into 6, inc} 6 times (48).

Rnd 9. {sc into 7, inc} 6 times (54).

Rnds 10–17. Sc into each (54).

Rnd 18. Sc into 16, hdc into next 4, sl st into next 2, hdc into next 2, dc into next 6, hdc into next 2, sl st into next 2, hdc into next 4, sc into next 16.

Rnd 19. Sc into 6, sl st into next.

Fasten off and leave a long tail for sewing. Place the hair on the head, secure it with pins, and sew it into place.

Make your own

GANDHI

Mohandas Karamchand Gandhi was one of the greatest
spiritual and political leaders of the twentieth century.
He is also honored by Indians as the father of the Indian
nation. Gandhi was a lawyer, a politician, and a social activist
who became the leader of the nationalist movement against
the British rule of India. He helped free the Indian people
through nonviolent resistance, which later inspired
civil rights activists, including Martin Luther King, Jr.
and Nelson Mandela.

MATERIALS

B-1 or C-2 (2.5 mm) crochet hook

$\frac{5}{16}$" (8 mm) safety eyes

Tapestry needle

Polyester fiberfill

Black thread for embroidery

Small amount of white felt

18 gauge (1 mm) floral stem wire

Round-nose pliers

YARNS

Scheepjes Catona 100% cotton yarn:

502 Camel—skin, 35 g

106 Snow White—dhoti, shawl, 20 g

507 Chocolate—shoes, 3 g

074 Mercury—moustache, 1 g

HEAD

Start with the skin color.

Rnd 1. 6 sc into magic ring (6).

Rnd 2. 2 sc into each (12).

Rnd 3. {sc, inc} 6 times (18).

Rnd 4. {sc into 2, inc} 6 times (24).

Rnd 5. {sc into 3, inc} 6 times (30).

Rnd 6. {sc into 4, inc} 6 times (36).

Rnd 7. {sc into 5, inc} 6 times (42).

Rnd 8. {sc into 6, inc} 6 times (48).

Rnd 9. {sc into 7, inc} 6 times (54).

Rnds 10–16. Sc into each (54).

Rnd 17. {sc into 8, inc} 6 times (60).

Rnds 18–20. Sc into each (60).

Rnd 21. {sc into 8, dec} 6 times (54).

Rnd 22. {sc into 7, dec} 6 times (48).

Rnd 23. {sc into 6, dec} 6 times (42).

Rnd 24. {sc into 5, dec} 6 times (36).

Add the eyes (see page 126 for guidance).

Rnd 25. {sc into 4, dec} 6 times (30).

Rnd 26. {sc into 3, dec} 6 times (24).

Start to stuff the head.

Rnd 27. {sc into 2, dec} 6 times (18).

Rnd 28. {sc, dec} 6 times (12).

Continue to stuff the head firmly.

Rnd 29. Sc into each FLO (12).

Do not fasten off, continue with the body.

BODY

Rnd 1. {sc, inc} 6 times (18).

Rnd 2. {sc into 2, inc} 6 times (24).

Rnd 3. Sc into each (24).

Rnd 4. {sc into 3, inc} 6 times (30).

Rnd 5. Sc into each (30).

Rnd 6. {sc into 4, inc} 6 times (36).

Rnds 7–10. Sc into each (36).

Rnd 11. Sc into each BLO (36).

Rnd 12. Sc into each (36).

Rnd 13. {sc into 16, dec} 2 times (34).

Rnds 14–15. Sc into each (34).

Do not fasten off, continue with the legs. Stuff the neck and body continuously.

LEGS

To make the legs, divide the work: 14 stitches for each of the legs, and 3 stitches between the legs, both front and back. Mark the stitches with yarn or a stitch marker. Make sure the legs line up with the eyes. If the last stitch of the body is within the 14 stitches for the legs, then continue crocheting. If it is within the 3 stitches, then fasten off, leave a tail for sewing later, and rejoin the skin-colored yarn with a sl st at the back of the doll.

Rnds 1–3. Sc into each (14).

Rnd 4. {sc into 5, dec} 2 times (12).

Rnds 5–8. Sc into each (12).

Stuff the body firmly and stuff the leg as you crochet it.

Rnd 9. {sc into 4, dec} 2 times (10).

Rnds 10–12. Sc into each (10).

Stuff the leg firmly.

Rnd 13. Dec 5 times (5).

Fasten off, sew up the small hole, and weave in the ends. For the second leg, rejoin with a sl st at the back of the doll and work the leg. When finished, sew up the hole between the legs. Weave in the ends.

DHOTI

Using the color of the dhoti, join with a sl st to a front loop of round 10 at the center back of the body. Work continuously, but join with a sl st at the end of each round. Ch 1 at the beginning does not count as sc.

Rnd 1. Ch 1, sc into each (36).

Rnd 2. Ch 1, BLO {sc into 2, inc} 12 times (48).

Rnds 3–11. Ch 1, BLO sc into each (48).

Fasten off and weave in the ends.

ARMS

Use the skin color, make two.

Rnd 1. 6 sc into magic ring (6).

Rnd 2. {sc, inc} 3 times (9).

Rnd 3. Sc into each (9).

Rnd 4. {sc into 2, dec} 2 times, sc into last (7).

Rnds 5–12. Sc into each (7).

Fasten off and leave a long tail for sewing. Position an arm on each side of the doll and sew them into place.

SHAWL

Use the color of the shawl. Use pins to mark the position of the shawl by placing two pins in line with the eyes into the front loops of round 1 of the dhoti, 10 stitches apart. Start crocheting from the right side, joining with a sl st to the front loop of round 1 of the dhoti at the first pin. Work in rows, turning at the end of each row. Ch 1 at the beginning does not count as sc.

Row 1. Sc into each front loop of round 1 of dhoti between pins, turn (10).

Row 2. Ch 1, sc into each, turn (10).

Row 3. Ch 1, sk first st, sc into 9, turn (9).

Row 4. Ch 1, sc into each, turn (9).

Row 5. Ch 1, sk first st, sc into 8, turn (8).

Row 6. Ch 1, sc into each, turn (8).

Row 7. Ch 1, sk first st, sc into 7, turn (7).

Row 8. Ch 1, sc into 5, dec, turn (6).

Row 9. Ch 1, sk first st, sc into 5, turn (5).

Row 10. Ch 1, sc into 3, dec, turn (4).

Row 11. Ch 1, sk first st, sc into 3, turn (3).

Row 12. Ch 1, sc, dec, turn (2).

Rows 13–16. Ch 1, sc into each, turn (2).

Row 17. Ch 1, inc, sc into last, turn (3).

Row 18. Ch 1, sc into 2, inc, turn (4).

Row 19. Ch 1, inc, sc into 3, turn (5).

Row 20. Ch 1, sc into 4, inc, turn (6).

Row 21. Ch 1, inc, sc into 5, turn (7).

Row 22. Ch 1, sc into 6, inc, turn (8).

Row 23. Ch 1, sc into each, turn (8).

Row 24. Ch 1, sc into 7, inc, turn (9).

Row 25. Ch 1, sc into each, turn (9).

Row 26. Ch 1, sc into 8, inc (10).

Fasten off and leave a long tail for sewing. Use two pins to secure the back part of the shawl onto the dhoti and sew it to the front loops of round 1.

FINISHING THE DHOTI

Crochet a strip using the color of the dhoti. Start by leaving a long tail.

Row 1. Ch 4, sc into 2nd ch from hook and next 2, turn (3).

Rows 2–24. Ch 1, sc into each, turn (3).

Fasten off and leave a long tail. Place the strip between the legs and sew it to round 1 of the dhoti on both front and back, right below the shawl. Weave in the ends.

EYEBROWS, NOSE, AND MUSTACHE

With skin-colored yarn, embroider the nose between rounds 18 and 19. Mark the position of the mustache with four pins. Place two pins on either side of the nose between rounds 19 and 20. Place two more pins between rounds 20 and 21 one stitch away from the previous pins. Using gray yarn, embroider the mustache between the pins. With black thread, embroider the eyebrows between rounds 13 and 15.

SHOES

Use the color of the shoes, make two.

Rnd 1. Ch 4, 2 sc into 2nd ch from hook, sc, 3 sc into next. Continue working on the other side of the foundation chain: sc, 2 sc into last (9).

Rnd 2. Inc 2 times, sc, inc 3 times, sc, inc 2 times (16).

Rnd 3. Sc into each BLO (16).

Rnd 4. Sc into 5, dec 3 times, sc into 5 (13).

Rnd 5. Sc into 6, dec, sc into 5 (12).

Fasten off and leave a long tail for sewing. Add stuffing to the toe of the shoes, position them on the legs, and sew them into place. Weave in the ends.

GLASSES

Take the floral wire and find a round object to use to form the ring shape for the glasses. I used the plastic part of a thread spool, with a ½" (1.5 cm) diameter. Wrap the longer end of the wire around the spool, leaving 1½" (4 cm) on the shorter end. Wrap the wire all the way around the spool. For the other ring of the glasses, measure 1¾" (4.5 cm) from the first ring on the longer end of the wire and wrap it around the spool again. Use the spool to shape the curved bridge of the glasses. Bend the stems at right angles and place the glasses on the doll. Insert the stems into the head four stitches away from the eyes between rounds 16 and 17.

Make your own

PRINCE

Genius, talent, composer, icon, inspiration, the purple master, visionary—just a few of Prince's qualities. Prince Rogers Nelson was an American singer-songwriter, a multi-instrumentalist, and one of the greatest musicians of his generation. Coming from a musical family, he played the piano by the age of seven and had a record deal by the age of nineteen. He always said that he was going to play all kinds of music, and not be judged for the color of his skin but for the quality of his work—and he remained true to himself. He was always on the cutting edge and his music integrated multiple styles, including funk, soul, pop, rock, R&B, and jazz. He was and still is an inspiration for musicians and entertainers of all ages and genres.

MATERIALS

B-1 or C-2 (2.5 mm) crochet hook

⁵⁄₁₆" (8 mm) safety eyes

Tapestry needle

Polyester fiberfill

Black thread for embroidery

Small amount of white felt

YARNS

Scheepjes Catona 100% cotton yarn:

503 Hazelnut—skin, 20 g

106 Snow White—shirt, 10 g

110 Jet Black—hair, pants, 50 g

113 Delphinium—coat, shoes, 18 g

HEAD

Start with the skin color.

Rnd 1. 6 sc into magic ring (6).

Rnd 2. 2 sc into each (12).

Rnd 3. {sc, inc} 6 times (18).

Rnd 4. {sc into 2, inc} 6 times (24).

Rnd 5. {sc into 3, inc} 6 times (30).

Rnd 6. {sc into 4, inc} 6 times (36).

Rnd 7. {sc into 5, inc} 6 times (42).

Rnd 8. {sc into 6, inc} 6 times (48).

Rnd 9. {sc into 7, inc} 6 times (54).

Rnds 10–16. Sc into each (54).

Rnd 17. {sc into 8, inc} 6 times (60).

Rnds 18–20. Sc into each (60).

Rnd 21. {sc into 8, dec} 6 times (54).

Rnd 22. {sc into 7, dec} 6 times (48).

Rnd 23. {sc into 6, dec} 6 times (42).

Rnd 24. {sc into 5, dec} 6 times (36).

Add the eyes (see page 126 for guidance).

Rnd 25. {sc into 4, dec} 6 times (30).

Rnd 26. {sc into 3, dec} 6 times (24).

Start to stuff the head.

Rnd 27. {sc into 2, dec} 6 times (18).

Rnd 28. {sc, dec} 6 times (12).

Continue to stuff the head firmly.

Rnd 29. Sc into each FLO (12).

Change to the color of the shirt.

BODY

Rnd 1. {sc, inc} 6 times (18).

Rnd 2. BLO {sc into 2, inc} 6 times (24).

Rnd 3. BLO sc into each (24).

Rnd 4. BLO {sc into 3, inc} 6 times (30).

Rnd 5. BLO sc into each (30).

Rnd 6. BLO {sc into 4, inc} 6 times (36).

Rnd 7. BLO sc into each (36).

Rnd 8. BLO sc into each (36).

Change to the color of the pants.

Rnds 9–12. Sc into each (36).

Rnd 13. {sc into 16, dec} 2 times (34).

Rnds 14–15. Sc into each (34).

Do not fasten off, continue with the legs. Stuff the neck and body continuously.

LEGS

To make the legs, divide the work: 14 stitches for each of the legs, and 3 stitches between the legs, both front and back. Mark the stitches with yarn or a stitch marker. Make sure the legs line up with the eyes. If the last stitch of the body is within the 14 stitches for the legs, then continue crocheting. If it is within the 3 stitches, then fasten off, leave a tail for sewing later, and rejoin the pants-colored yarn with a sl st at the back of the doll.

Rnds 1–3. Sc into each (14).

Rnd 4. {sc into 5, dec} 2 times (12).

Rnds 5–8. Sc into each (12).

Stuff the body firmly and stuff the leg as you crochet it.

Rnd 9. {sc into 4, dec} 2 times BLO (10).

Rnds 10–12. Sc into each (10).

Stuff the leg firmly.

Rnd 13. Dec 5 times (5).

Fasten off, sew up the small hole, and weave in the ends. For the second leg, rejoin with a sl st at the back of the doll and work the leg. When finished, sew up the hole between the legs. Weave in the ends.

PANTS

To make the bell-bottom flares, join the black yarn with a sl st to a front loop of round 8 at the back of one leg.

Rnd 1. Ch 1, {sc, inc} 6 times (18).

Rnds 2–4. Sc into each (18).

Fasten off, weave in the ends, and repeat with the other leg.

SHOES

Use the color of the shoes, make two.

Rnd 1. Ch 4, 2 sc into 2nd ch from hook, sc,

3 sc into next. Continue working on the other side of the foundation chain: sc, 2 sc into last (9).

Rnd 2. Inc 2 times, sc, inc 3 times, sc, inc 2 times (16).

Rnd 3. Sc into each BLO (16).

Rnd 4. Sc into 5, dec 3 times, sc into 5 (13).

Rnd 5. Sc into 6, dec, sc into 5 (12).

Fasten off and leave a long tail for sewing. Add stuffing to the toe of the shoes, turn up the bottom of the pants, position the shoes on the legs, and sew them into place. Weave in the ends.

SHIRT NECK FRILLS

Use the color of the shirt, make three.

Ch 4, 3 hdc into 3rd ch from hook, 3 hdc into last, ch 2, sl st into same st. Fasten off and leave a long tail for sewing. Sew the frills onto the front loops of the shirt in line with the nose. Sew the first frill onto the front loops of round 3, the second onto round 2, and the last onto round 1. Weave in the ends.

EYEBROWS, NOSE, AND MUSTACHE

Using black thread, embroider the eyebrows between rounds 13 and 15. With skin-colored yarn, embroider the nose between rounds 18 and 19. Mark the position of the mustache with four pins. Place two pins next to each other below the nose between rounds 19 and 20. Place two more pins one round below and two stitches away from the previous pins. Using black thread, embroider a thin line between the two sets of pins.

COAT

Use the color of the coat. Work in rows, turning at the end of each row. Ch 1 at the beginning does not count as sc.

Row 1. Ch 19, sc into 2nd ch from hook and next 17, turn (18).

Row 2. Ch 1, sc, {inc, sc into 4} 3 times, inc, sc into last, turn (22).

Row 3. Ch 1, sc into each, turn (22).

Row 4. Ch 1, sc, {inc, sc into 5} 3 times, inc, sc into last 2, turn (26).

Row 5. Ch 1, sc into each, turn (26).

Row 6. Ch 1, sc into 2, {inc, sc into 3} 6 times, turn (32).

Rows 7–11. Ch 1, sc into each, turn (32).

Row 12. Ch 1, sc into 2, {inc, sc into 6} 4 times, inc, sc into last, turn (37).

Rows 13–18. Ch 1, sc into each, turn (37).

Row 19. Ch 1, twisted sc (see page 122) into each (37). Place the coat in front of you with the right side facing out. Join the purple yarn with a sl st to the very first row of the coat, and crochet twisted sc into each st. Fasten off and leave a long tail for sewing. Fold the upper part of the coat to form a collar and place the coat on the doll. Secure it with pins and stitch it onto the body on both sides next to the shirt frills.

ARMS

Start with the skin color, make two.

Rnd 1. 6 sc into magic ring (6).

Rnd 2. {sc, inc} 3 times (9).

Rnd 3. Sc into each (9).

Rnd 4. {sc into 2, dec} 2 times, sc into last (7).

Rnd 5. Sc into each (7).

Change to the color of the coat.

Rnd 6. Sc into each BLO (7).

Rnds 7–12. Sc into each (7).

Fasten off and leave a long tail for sewing.

SHIRT CUFFS

Use the color of the shirt, make two.

Join with a sl st to a front loop of round 5 of the arm.
Ch 2, 2 dc into same front loop, 3 dc into each of next
6 front loops, join with a sl st to first dc. Fasten off and
weave in the ends. Position an arm on each side of the
doll and sew them into place.

HAIR

Use the hair color and a piece of yarn or a stitch marker
for marking the rounds as you are crocheting the main
part of the hair. Leave the marker in place because you will
need it when you are crocheting the curls.

Rnd 1. 6 sc into magic ring (6).

Rnd 2. 2 sc in each st (12).

Rnd 3. {sc, inc} 6 times BLO (18).

Rnd 4. {sc into 2, inc} 6 times (24).

Rnd 5. {sc into 3, inc} 6 times BLO (30).

Rnd 6. {sc into 4, inc} 6 times (36).

Rnd 7. {sc into 5, inc} 6 times BLO (42).

Rnd 8. {sc into 6, inc} 6 times (48).

Rnd 9. {sc into 7, inc} 6 times BLO (54).

Rnd 10. Sc into each (54).

Rnd 11. Sc into each BLO (54).

Rnd 12. Sc into each (54).

Rnd 13. Sc into each BLO (54).

Rnd 14. Sc into each (54).

Rnd 15. Sc into each BLO (54).

Rnd 16. Sc into each (54).

Rnd 17. Sc into each BLO (54).

Rnd 18. Sc into each (54).

Rnd 19. Sc into each BLO (54).

Do not fasten off. You will now crochet the curls by
working into the front loops of rounds 18 to 2 of the hair.

CURLS

Front loops of Rnd 18: Ch 1, sl st into first front loop,
ch 9, sc into 2nd ch from hook, {inc, sc} 3 times, inc into
last. Sl st into next 3 front loops on the wig.

Ch 11, sc into 2nd ch from hook, {inc, sc} 4 times, inc
into last. Sl st into next 3 front loops on the wig.

Ch 13, sc into 2nd ch from hook, {inc, sc} 5 times, inc
into last. Sl st into next 3 front loops on the wig.

Ch 11, sc into 2nd ch from hook, {inc, sc} 4 times, inc
into last. Sl st into next 3 front loops on the wig.

Ch 9, sc into 2nd ch from hook, {inc, sc} 3 times, inc
into last. Sl st into next 3 front loops on the wig.

[Ch 7, sc into 2nd ch from hook, {inc, sc} 2 times, inc
into last. Sl st into next 3 front loops on the wig] 3 times.

Ch 11, sc into 2nd ch from hook, {inc, sc} 4 times, inc
into last. Sl st into next 3 front loops on the wig.

[Ch 9, sc into 2nd ch from hook, {inc, sc} 3 times, inc
into last. Sl st into next 3 front loops on the wig] 3 times.

Ch 11, sc into 2nd ch from hook, {inc, sc} 4 times, inc
into last. Sl st into next 3 front loops on the wig.

[Ch 7, sc into 2nd ch from hook, {inc, sc} 2 times, inc
into last. Sl st into next 3 front loops on the wig] 4 times.
Sl st into last 4 front loops on the wig (17 curls).

Front loops of Rnd 16: Sl st into first 2 front loops,
ch 11, sc into 2nd ch from hook, {inc, sc} 4 times, inc
into last. Sl st into next 3 front loops on the wig.

Ch 13, sc into 2nd ch from hook, {inc, sc} 5 times, inc
into last. Sl st into next 3 front loops on the wig.

[Ch 15, sc into 2nd ch from hook, {inc, sc} 6 times, inc
into last. Sl st into next 3 front loops on the wig] 2 times.

Ch 11, sc into 2nd ch from hook, {inc, sc} 4 times, inc
into last. Sl st into next 3 front loops on the wig.

[Ch 7, sc into 2nd ch from hook, {inc, sc} 2 times, inc
into last. Sl st into next 3 front loops on the wig] 3 times.

Ch 11, sc into 2nd ch from hook, {inc, sc} 4 times, inc
into last. Sl st into next 3 front loops on the wig.

[Ch 9, sc into 2nd ch from hook, {inc, sc} 3 times, inc
into last. Sl st into next 3 front loops on the wig] 3 times.

Ch 11, sc into 2nd ch from hook, {inc, sc} 4 times, inc
into last. Sl st into next 3 front loops on the wig.

[Ch 7, sc into 2nd ch from hook, {inc, sc} 2 times, inc into last. Sl st into next 3 front loops on the wig] 4 times. Sl st into last 4 front loops on the wig (17 curls).

Front loops of Rnd 14: Repeat Rnd 16.

Front loops of Rnd 12: Sl st into first 2 front loops, ch 11, sc into 2nd ch from hook, {inc, sc} 4 times, inc into last. Sl st into next 3 front loops on the wig.
[Ch 13, sc into 2nd ch from hook, {inc, sc} 5 times, inc into last. Sl st into next 3 front loops on the wig] 3 times.
Ch 9, sc into 2nd ch from hook, {inc, sc} 3 times, inc into last. Sl st into next 3 front loops on the wig.
[Ch 7, sc into 2nd ch from hook, {inc, sc} 2 times, inc into last. Sl st into next 3 front loops on the wig] 3 times.
[Ch 9, sc into 2nd ch from hook, {inc, sc} 3 times, inc into last. Sl st into next 3 front loops on the wig] 5 times.
[Ch 7, sc into 2nd ch from hook, {inc, sc} 2 times, inc into last. Sl st into next 3 front loops on the wig] 4 times. Sl st into last 4 front loops on the wig (17 curls).

Front loops of Rnd 10: Repeat Rnd 12.

Front loops of Rnd 8: Sl st into first front loop, [ch 11, sc into 2nd ch from hook, {inc, sc} 4 times, inc into last. Sl st into next 3 front loops on the wig] 3 times. Ch 9, sc into 2nd ch from hook, {inc, sc} 3 times, inc into last. Sl st into next 3 front loops on the wig. [Ch 7, sc into 2nd ch from hook, {inc, sc} 2 times, inc into last. Sl st into next 3 front loops on the wig] 10 times. Sl st into last 5 front loops on the wig (14 curls).

Front loops of Rnd 6: Sl st into first front loop, [ch 9, sc into 2nd ch from hook, {inc, sc} 3 times, inc into last. Sl st into next 3 front loops on the wig] 3 times. [Ch 7, sc into 2nd ch from hook, {inc, sc} 2 times, inc into last. Sl st into next 3 front loops on the wig] 8 times. Sl st into last 5 front loops on the wig (14 curls).

Front loops of Rnd 4: Sl st into the first front loop, [ch 7, sc into 2nd ch from hook, {inc, sc} 2 times, inc into last. Sl st into next 3 front loops on the wig] 7 times. Sl st into last 5 front loops on the wig (7 curls).

Front loops of Rnd 2: Sl st into first front loop, [ch 7, sc into 2nd ch from hook, {inc, sc} 2 times, inc into last. Sl st into next 3 front loops on the wig] 4 times. Sl st into last 5 front loops on the wig (4 curls).

Fasten off and leave a long tail for sewing. Place the hair on the head, secure it with pins, and sew it into place.

Make your own

KATHERINE JOHNSON

Katherine Johnson was an American mathematician. She graduated summa cum laude from college at the age of eighteen with degrees in mathematics and French. She became a teacher, but left the profession to start a family. When her three daughters were older, she became one of the first African-American women to work as a NASA scientist. She helped to make it possible for John Glenn to be the first American to orbit the Earth. And in 1969 she calculated the precise trajectories that would allow Apollo 11—with Neil Armstrong on board—to land on the Moon and safely return to Earth.

MATERIALS

B-1 or C-2 (2.5 mm) crochet hook

⁵⁄₁₆" (8 mm) safety eyes

Tapestry needle

Polyester fiberfill

Black thread for embroidery

Small amount of white felt

18 gauge (1 mm) floral stem wire

Round-nose pliers

YARNS

Scheepjes Catona 100% cotton yarn:

507 Chocolate—skin, 22 g

510 Sky Blue—dress, 25 g

106 Snow White—stripes on dress, 4 g

110 Jet Black—hair, 20 g

248 Champagne—shoes, 3 g

HEAD

Start with the skin color.

Rnd 1. 6 sc into magic ring (6).

Rnd 2. 2 sc into each (12).

Rnd 3. {sc, inc} 6 times (18).

Rnd 4. {sc into 2, inc} 6 times (24).

Rnd 5. {sc into 3, inc} 6 times (30).

Rnd 6. {sc into 4, inc} 6 times (36).

Rnd 7. {sc into 5, inc} 6 times (42).

Rnd 8. {sc into 6, inc} 6 times (48).

Rnd 9. {sc into 7, inc} 6 times (54).

Rnds 10–16. Sc into each (54).

Rnd 17. {sc into 8, inc} 6 times (60).

Rnds 18–20. Sc into each (60).

Rnd 21. {sc into 8, dec} 6 times (54).

Rnd 22. {sc into 7, dec} 6 times (48).

Rnd 23. {sc into 6, dec} 6 times (42).

Rnd 24. {sc into 5, dec} 6 times (36).

Add the eyes (see page 126 for guidance).

Rnd 25. {sc into 4, dec} 6 times (30).

Rnd 26. {sc into 3, dec} 6 times (24).

Start to stuff the head.

Rnd 27. {sc into 2, dec} 6 times (18).

Rnd 28. {sc, dec} 6 times (12).

Continue to stuff the head firmly.

Rnd 29. Sc into each FLO (12).

Change to the color of the dress.

BODY

Rnd 1. {sc, inc} 6 times (18).

Rnd 2. {sc into 2, inc} 6 times (24).

Rnd 3. Sc into each (24).

Rnd 4. {sc into 3, inc} 6 times (30).

Rnd 5. Sc into each (30).

Rnd 6. {sc into 4, inc} 6 times (36).

Rnd 7. Sc into each (36).

Rnd 8. Sc into each (36).

Rnd 9. Sc into each (36).

Change to the skin color.

Rnd 10. Sc into each BLO (36).

Rnds 11–12. Sc into each (36).

Rnd 13. {sc into 16, dec} 2 times (34).

Rnds 14–15. Sc into each (34).

Do not fasten off, continue with the legs. Stuff the neck and body continuously.

LEGS

To make the legs, divide the work: 14 stitches for each of the legs, and 3 stitches between the legs, both front and back. Mark the stitches with yarn or a stitch marker. Make sure the legs line up with the eyes. If the last stitch of the body is within the 14 stitches for the legs, then continue crocheting. If it is within the 3 stitches, then fasten off, leave a tail for sewing later, and rejoin the skin-colored yarn with a sl st at the back of the doll.

Rnds 1–3. Sc into each (14).

Rnd 4. {sc into 5, dec} 2 times (12).

Rnds 5–8. Sc into each (12).

Stuff the body firmly and stuff the leg as you crochet it.

Rnd 9. {sc into 4, dec} 2 times (10).

Rnds 10–12. Sc into each (10).

Stuff the leg firmly.

Rnd 13. Dec 5 times (5).

Fasten off, sew up the small hole, and weave in the ends. For the second leg, rejoin with a sl st at the back of the doll and work the leg. When finished, sew up the hole between the legs. Weave in the ends.

SKIRT

Using the color of the dress, join with a sl st to a front loop of round 9 at the center back of the body. Work continuously, but join with a sl st at the end of each round. Ch 2 at the beginning does not count as dc.

Rnd 1. Ch 2, 2 dc into each (72).

Rnd 2. Ch 2, 2 dc into each (144).

Rnds 3–6. Ch 2, dc into each (144).

Change to white yarn for the stripe around the hem of the skirt. Turn the doll upside down and crochet slip stitches into the last round from the wrong side of the skirt. Fasten off and weave in the ends.

EYEBROWS AND NOSE

Using black thread, embroider the eyebrows between rounds 12 and 14. With skin-colored yarn, embroider the nose between rounds 18 and 19.

ARMS

Use the skin color, make two.

Rnd 1. 6 sc into magic ring (6).

Rnd 2. {sc, inc} 3 times (9).

Rnd 3. Sc into each (9).

Rnd 4. {sc into 1, dec} 3 times (6).

Rnds 5–12. Sc into each (6).

Fasten off and leave a long tail for sewing. Sew up the hole and weave in the ends.

SHIRT SLEEVES

Use the color of the dress, make two.

Rnd 1. 6 sc into magic ring (6).

Rnd 2. {sc, inc} 3 times (9).

Rnds 3–4. Sc into each (9).

Change to white yarn and crochet slip stitches into the last round from the wrong side of the sleeve. Fasten off and leave a long tail for sewing. Place the arms into the sleeves. Using small stitches, sew the sleeves onto the arms. Sew the sleeved arms onto the body. Weave in the ends.

SHOES

Use the color of the shoes, make two.

Rnd 1. Ch 4, 2 sc into 2nd ch from hook, sc, 3 sc into next. Continue working on the other side of the foundation chain: sc, 2 sc into last (9).

Rnd 2. Inc 2 times, sc, inc 3 times, sc, inc 2 times (16).

Rnd 3. Sc into each BLO (16).

Rnd 4. Sc into 5, dec 3 times, sc into 5 (13).

Rnd 5. Sc into 6, dec, sc into 5 (12).

Fasten off and leave a long tail for sewing. Add stuffing to the toe of the shoes, position them on the legs, and sew them into place. Weave in the ends.

HAIR

Use the hair color.

Rnd 1. 6 sc into magic ring (6).

Rnd 2. 2 sc into each (12).

Rnd 3. {sc, inc} 6 times (18).

Rnd 4. {sc into 2, inc} 6 times (24).

Rnd 5. {sc into 3, inc} 6 times (30).

Rnd 6. {sc into 4, inc} 6 times (36).

Rnd 7. {sc into 5, inc} 6 times (42).

Rnd 8. {sc into 6, inc} 6 times (48).

Rnd 9. {sc into 7, inc} 6 times (54).

Rnds 10–15. Sc into each (54).

Rnd 16. Sc, 3 hdc into next, sc into 25, 3 hdc into next, sc into 26 (58).

Rnd 17. Sc into 2, 3 hdc into next, sc into 27, 3 hdc into next, sc into 27 (62).

Rnd 18. Hdc into next 3, 3 hdc into next, sc into 29, 3 hdc into next, hdc into 28 (66).

Rnd 19. Hdc into 4, 3 hdc into next, sc into 9, sl st into next, and continue with the curls:

★ Ch 10, sc into 2nd ch from hook, {inc, sc into next} 4 times, inc into last. Sl st into next 2 on the hair. Repeat from ★ 6 times. For the last curl, crochet only one sl st on the hair. Continue on the hair:

Sc into 8, 3 hdc into next, hdc into 29. Join with sl st into first st of round 19.

Fasten off and leave a long tail for sewing. Place the hair on the head, secure it with pins, and sew it into place.

GLASSES

Take the floral wire and find a round object to use to form the ring shape for the glasses. I used the plastic part of a thread spool, with a ¾" (2 cm) diameter. Wrap the longer end of the wire around the spool, leaving 1½" (4 cm) on the shorter end. Wrap the wire all the way around the spool. For the other ring of the glasses, measure 1¾" (4.5 cm) from the first ring on the longer end of the wire and wrap it around the spool again. Use the spool to shape the curved bridge of the glasses. Bend the stems at right angles and place the glasses on the doll. Insert the stems into the head four stitches away from the eyes between rounds 16 and 17, below the hair.

Make your own

ABRAHAM LINCOLN

Abraham Lincoln was the sixteenth president of the
United States of America. He served as president for five
years, until his assassination in 1865. He was self-educated,
and though he was born in poverty, he became a successful
lawyer, Illinois state legislator, and a US congressman.
As a president he is best known for leading the country
during the Civil War and keeping the country united. He
also pushed to end slavery by issuing the Emancipation
Proclamation and, later, the Thirteenth Amendment, which
outlawed slavery and freed all slaves in the United States.

MATERIALS

B-1 or C-2 (2.5mm) crochet hook

5⁄16" (8 mm) safety eyes

Tapestry needle

Polyester fiberfill

Black thread for embroidery

Small amount of white felt

YARNS

Scheepjes Catona 100% cotton yarn:

130 Old Lace—skin, 20 g

106 Snow White—shirt, 10 g

074 Mercury—pants, 10 g

110 Jet Black—hat, coat, shoes, 35 g

507 Chocolate—hair, 18 g

HEAD

Start with the skin color.

Rnd 1. 6 sc into magic ring (6).

Rnd 2. 2 sc into each (12).

Rnd 3. {sc, inc} 6 times (18).

Rnd 4. {sc into 2, inc} 6 times (24).

Rnd 5. {sc into 3, inc} 6 times (30).

Rnd 6. {sc into 4, inc} 6 times (36).

Rnd 7. {sc into 5, inc} 6 times (42).

Rnd 8. {sc into 6, inc} 6 times (48).

Rnd 9. {sc into 7, inc} 6 times (54).

Rnds 10–16. Sc into each (54).

Rnd 17. {sc into 8, inc} 6 times (60).

Rnds 18–20. Sc into each (60).

Rnd 21. {sc into 8, dec} 6 times (54).

Rnd 22. {sc into 7, dec} 6 times (48).

Rnd 23. {sc into 6, dec} 6 times (42).

Rnd 24. {sc into 5, dec} 6 times (36).

Add the eyes (see page 126 for guidance).

Rnd 25. {sc into 4, dec} 6 times (30).

Rnd 26. {sc into 3, dec} 6 times (24).

Start to stuff the head.

Rnd 27. {sc into 2, dec} 6 times (18).

Rnd 28. {sc, dec} 6 times (12).

Continue to stuff the head firmly.

Rnd 29. Sc into each FLO (12).

Change to the color of the shirt.

BODY

Rnd 1. {sc, inc} 6 times (18).

Rnd 2. BLO {sc into 2, inc} 6 times (24).

Rnd 3. BLO sc into each (24).

Rnd 4. BLO {sc into 3, inc} 6 times (30).

Rnd 5. BLO sc into each (30).

Rnd 6. BLO {sc into 4, inc} 6 times (36).

Rnd 7. BLO sc into each (36).

Rnd 8. BLO sc into each (36).

Rnd 9. BLO sc into each (36).

Change to the color of the pants.

Rnd 10. Sc into each BLO (36).

Rnds 11–12. Sc into each (36).

Rnd 13. {sc into 16, dec} 2 times (34).

Rnds 14–15. Sc into each (34).

Do not fasten off, continue with the legs. Stuff the neck and body continuously.

LEGS

To make the legs, divide the work: 14 stitches for each of the legs, and 3 stitches between the legs, both front and back. Mark the stitches with yarn or a stitch marker. Make sure the legs line up with the eyes. If the last stitch of the body is within the 14 stitches for the legs, then continue crocheting. If it is within the 3 stitches, then fasten off, leave a tail for sewing later, and rejoin the pants-colored yarn with a sl st at the back of the doll.

Rnds 1–3. Sc into each (14).

Rnd 4. {sc into 5, dec} 2 times (12).

Rnds 5–8. Sc into each (12).

Stuff the body firmly and stuff the leg as you crochet it.

Rnd 9. {sc into 4, dec} 2 times (10).

Change to the skin color.

Rnd 10. Sc into each BLO (10).

Rnds 11–12. Sc into each (10).

Stuff the leg firmly.

Rnd 13. Dec 5 times (5).

Fasten off, sew up the small hole, and weave in the ends. For the second leg, rejoin with a sl st at the back of the doll and work the leg. When finished, sew up the hole between the legs. Weave in the ends. With the color of the pants, rejoin with a sl st in the front loop of round 9 at the back of the leg. Crochet slip stitches into each front loop. Fasten off and weave in the ends.

EYEBROWS AND NOSE

Using black thread, embroider the eyebrows between rounds 13 and 15. With skin-colored yarn, embroider the nose between rounds 18 and 19.

SHOES

Use the color of the shoes, make two.

Rnd 1. Ch 4, 2 sc into 2nd ch from hook, sc, 3 sc into next. Continue working on the other side of the foundation chain: sc, 2 sc into last (9).

Rnd 2. Inc 2 times, sc, inc 3 times, sc, inc 2 times (16).

Rnd 3. Sc into each BLO (16).

Rnd 4. Sc into 5, dec 3 times, sc into 5 (13).

Rnd 5. Sc into 6, dec, sc into 5 (12).

Fasten off and leave a long tail for sewing. Add stuffing to the toe of the shoes, position them on the legs, and sew them into place. Weave in the ends.

COAT

Use the color of the coat.

Work in rows, turning at the end of each row. Ch 1 at the beginning does not count as sc.

Row 1. Ch 21, sc into 2nd ch from hook and next 19, turn (20).

Row 2. Ch 1, sc into 2, {inc, sc into 4} 3 times, inc, sc into 2, turn (24).

Row 3. Ch 1, sc into each, turn (24).

Row 4. Sc into 2, {inc, sc into 5} 3 times, inc, sc into 3, turn (28).

Row 5. Sc into each, turn (28).

Row 6. Sc, {inc, sc into 4} 5 times, inc, sc into last, turn (34).

Rows 7–18. Sc into each, turn (34).

Row 19. Twisted sc (see page 122) into each (49).

Fasten off and weave in the ends. Fold the upper part of the coat to form a collar and place it onto the body of the doll. Cross the edges of the coat on the belly of the doll. Secure it with pins and sew it to the body.

ARMS

Start with the skin color, make two.

Rnd 1. 6 sc into magic ring (6).

Rnd 2. {sc, inc} 3 times (9).

Rnd 3. Sc into each (9).

Rnd 4. {sc into 2, dec} 2 times, sc into last (7).

Change to the color of the coat.

Rnds 5–12. Sc into each (7).

Fasten off and leave a long tail for sewing. Position an arm on each side of the doll and sew them into place.

BEARD

Use the hair color and work in rows.

Row 1. Ch 30, hdc into 3rd ch from hook and next 7, dc into next 12, hdc into next 8, turn. (28).

Row 2. Ch 1, {sc, inc} 4 times, hdc into next 12, {inc, sc} 4 times (36).

Fasten off and leave a long tail for sewing. Place the ends of the beard between rounds 15 and 16 on both sides of the head. The upper part of the beard should be between rounds 22 and 23. Sew it onto the face by the upper edge of the beard.

HAIR

Use the hair color.

Rnd 1. 6 sc into magic ring (6).

Rnd 2. 2 sc into each (12).

Rnd 3. {sc, inc} 6 times (18).

Rnd 4. {sc into 2, inc} 6 times (24).

Rnd 5. {sc into 3, inc} 6 times (30).

Rnd 6. {sc into 4, inc} 6 times (36).

Rnd 7. {sc into 5, inc} 6 times (42).

Rnd 8. {sc into 6, inc} 6 times (48).

Rnd 9. {sc into 7, inc} 6 times (54).

Rnds 10–17. Sc into each (54).

Rnd 18. Sl st into 2, hdc into next 2, dc into next 48, hdc into next, sc into last (54). Join with a sl st to first st of round 18.

Fasten off and leave a long tail for sewing. Place the hair on the head, making sure that the hair covers the ends of the beard. Secure it with pins and sew it into place.

HAT

Use the color of the hat.

Rnd 1. 7 sc into magic ring (7).

Rnd 2. 2 sc into each (14).

Rnd 3. {sc, inc} 7 times (21).

Rnd 4. {sc into 2, inc} 7 times (28).

Rnd 5. {sc into 3, inc} 7 times (35).

Rnd 6. {sc into 4, inc} 7 times (42).

Rnd 7. {sc into 5, inc} 7 times (49).

Rnd 8. {sc into 6, inc} 7 times (56).

Rnd 9. {sc into 7, inc} 7 times (63).

Rnd 10. Sc into each (63).

Rnd 11. Sc into each BLO (63).

Rnds 12–18. Sc into each (63).

Rnd 19. Sc into each (63). Join with a sl st to first st.

Rnd 20. Ch 2, FLO {dc into 2, inc} 21 times (84). Join with a sl st into first st.

Rnd 21. Sl st into each. (84)

Fasten off and weave in the ends. Add stuffing to the hat, place it on the head, and sew it into place.

Make your own

PABLO PICASSO

Pablo Picasso was a prolific Spanish painter and sculptor—undoubtedly one of the most influential artists of the twentieth century. Besides his more than twenty thousand paintings, drawings, sculptures, and ceramics, he is also known for cofounding the Cubist art movement and for the coinvention of collage. His undisputed talent, eccentric style, and free spirit made him the father of modern art.

MATERIALS

B-1 or C-2 (2.5 mm) crochet hook

⁵⁄₁₆" (8 mm) safety eyes

Tapestry needle

Polyester fiberfill

Black thread for embroidery

Small amount of white felt

YARNS

Scheepjes Catona 100% cotton yarn:

505 Linen—skin, 20 g

106 Snow White—shirt, 5 g

110 Jet Black—shirt, shoes, 8 g

503 Hazelnut—pants, 10 g

Scheepjes Softly yarn:

494 White—hair, 8 g

HEAD

Start with the skin color.

Rnd 1. 6 sc into magic ring (6).

Rnd 2. 2 sc into each (12).

Rnd 3. {sc, inc} 6 times (18).

Rnd 4. {sc into 2, inc} 6 times (24).

Rnd 5. {sc into 3, inc} 6 times (30).

Rnd 6. {sc into 4, inc} 6 times (36).

Rnd 7. {sc into 5, inc} 6 times (42).

Rnd 8. {sc into 6, inc} 6 times (48).

Rnd 9. {sc into 7, inc} 6 times (54).

Rnds 10–15. Sc into each (54).

Rnd 16. Sc into 28 BLO, sc into 26 (54).

Rnd 17. {sc into 8, inc} 4 times, place stitch marker for first safety eye, {sc into 8, inc}, sc into next, place stitch marker for second safety eye, sc into 7, inc (60).

Rnd 18. Sc into 31 BLO, sc into 29 (60).

Rnd 19. Sc into each (60).

Rnd 20. Sc into 31 BLO, sc into 29 (60).

Rnd 21. {sc into 8, dec} 6 times (54).

Rnd 22. Sc into next, sc into 6 BLO, dec BLO, {sc into 7, dec} 2 times BLO, {sc into 7, dec} 3 times (48).

Rnd 23. {sc into 6, dec} 6 times (42).

Rnd 24. {sc into 5, dec} 6 times (36).

Add the eyes (see page 126 for guidance).

Rnd 25. {sc into 4, dec} 6 times (30).

Rnd 26. {sc into 3, dec} 6 times (24).

Start to stuff the head.

Rnd 27. {sc into 2, dec} 6 times (18).

Rnd 28. {sc, dec} 6 times (12).

Continue to stuff the head firmly.

Rnd 29. Sc into each FLO (12).

Fasten off and weave in the ends.

HAIR

Use the hair color. Turn the head upside down, and ★ join with a sl st to the front loop of round 21 of the head. Crochet sc into each of the front loops of round 21.

After the last front loop, fasten off and weave in the ends. Repeat from ★ into the front loops of rounds 19, 17, and 15 of the head.

BODY

Start with the black shirt yarn. Join with a sl st to the center back of the neck. Work in continuous rounds but join with a sl st at the end of each round when you change colors. Ch 1 at the beginning does not count as sc.

Rnd 1. Ch 1, {sc, inc} 6 times (18). Change to the white shirt yarn.

Rnd 2. Ch 1, {sc into 2, inc} 6 times (24). Change to black.

Rnd 3. Ch 1, sc into each (24). Change to white.

Rnd 4. Ch 1, {sc into 3, inc} 6 times (30). Change to black.

Rnd 5. Ch 1, sc into each (30). Change to white.

Rnd 6. Ch 1, {sc into 4, inc} 6 times (36). Change to black.

Rnd 7. Ch 1, sc into each (36). Change to white.

Rnd 8. Ch 1, sc into each (36). Change to black, fasten off white.

Rnd 9. Ch 1, sc into each (36).

Change to the color of the trousers.

Rnd 10. Sc into each BLO (36).

Rnds 11–12. Sc into each (36).

Rnd 13. {sc into 16, dec} 2 times (34).

Rnds 14–15. Sc into each (34).

Do not fasten off, continue with the legs. Stuff the neck and body continuously.

LEGS

To make the legs, divide the work: 14 stitches for each of the legs, and 3 stitches between the legs, both front and back. Mark the stitches with yarn or a stitch marker. Make sure the legs line up with the eyes. If the last stitch of the body is within the 14 stitches for the legs, then continue crocheting. If it is within the 3 stitches, then fasten off, leave a tail for sewing later, and rejoin the pants-colored yarn with a sl st at the back of the doll.

Rnds 1–3. Sc into each (14).

Rnd 4. {sc into 5, dec} 2 times (12).

Rnds 5–8. Sc into each (12).

Stuff the body firmly and stuff the leg as you crochet it.

Rnd 9. {sc into 4, dec} 2 times (10).

Change to the skin color.

Rnd 10. Sc into each BLO (10).

Rnds 11–12. Sc into each (10).

Stuff the leg firmly.

Rnd 13. Dec 5 times (5).

Fasten off, sew up the small hole, and weave in the ends. For the second leg, rejoin with a sl st at the back of the doll and work the leg. When finished, sew up the hole between the legs. Weave in the ends.

PANT CUFFS

Use the color of the pants, make two.

Join with a sl st to the front loop of round 9 of the leg, sl st into each front loop. Fasten off and weave in the ends. Repeat for the second leg.

SHIRT EDGING

With black yarn, join with a slip stitch to the front loop of round 9 of the body, sl st into each front loop. Fasten off and weave in the ends.

EYEBROWS AND NOSE

Using black thread, embroider the eyebrows between rounds 13 and 15. With skin-colored yarn, embroider the nose between rounds 18 and 19.

ARMS

Start with the skin color, make two.

Rnd 1. 6 sc into magic ring (6).

Rnd 2. {sc, inc} 3 times (9).

Rnd 3. Sc into each (9).

Rnd 4. {sc into 2, dec} 2 times, sc into last (7).

Rnds 5–8. Sc into each (7). Change to black yarn.

Rnd 9. Sc into each (7). Change to white yarn.

Rnd 10. Sc into each (7). Change to black yarn.

Rnd 11. Sc into each (7). Change to white yarn.

Rnd 12. Sc into each (7).

Fasten off and leave a long tail for sewing. Position an arm on each side of the doll at round 2 of the body and sew them into place.

SHOES

Use the color of the shoes, make two.

Rnd 1. Ch 4, 2 sc into 2nd ch from hook, sc, 3 sc into next. Continue working on the other side of the foundation chain: sc, 2 sc into last (9).

Rnd 2. Inc 2 times, sc, inc 3 times, sc, inc 2 times (16).

Rnd 3. Sc into each BLO (16).

Rnd 4. Sc into 5, dec 3 times, sc into 5 (13).

Rnd 5. Sc into 6, dec, sc into 5 (12).

Fasten off and leave a long tail for sewing. Add stuffing to the toe of the shoes, position them on the legs, and sew them into place. Weave in the ends.

Make your own

ROSA PARKS

Rosa Parks was an American activist in the civil rights movement. On December 1, 1955, she was arrested for refusing to give up her seat to a white passenger on a segregated bus in Montgomery, Alabama. Though she was not the first person to resist bus segregation, her brave move led to the Montgomery bus boycott, during which the black community refused to use the Montgomery buses for over a year. The boycott ended when the US Supreme Court ruled that bus segregation was unconstitutional. Parks later moved to Detroit and continued to fight to end racial injustice for the rest of her life.

MATERIALS

B-1 or C-2 (2.5 mm) crochet hook

5/16" (8 mm) safety eyes

Tapestry needle

Polyester fiberfill

Black thread for embroidery

Small amount of white felt

18 gauge (1 mm) floral stem wire

Round-nose pliers

YARNS

Scheepjes Catona 100% cotton yarn:

503 Hazelnut—skin, 22 g

106 Snow White—shirt, flower, 10 g

391 Deep Ocean Green—skirt, coat, 25 g

528 Silver Blue—suit edging, hat, 12 g

110 Jet Black—hair, 20 g

162 Black Coffee—shoes, 3 g

HEAD

Start with the skin color.

Rnd 1. 6 sc into magic ring (6).

Rnd 2. 2 sc into each (12).

Rnd 3. {sc, inc} 6 times (18).

Rnd 4. {sc into 2, inc} 6 times (24).

Rnd 5. {sc into 3, inc} 6 times (30).

Rnd 6. {sc into 4, inc} 6 times (36).

Rnd 7. {sc into 5, inc} 6 times (42).

Rnd 8. {sc into 6, inc} 6 times (48).

Rnd 9. {sc into 7, inc} 6 times (54).

Rnds 10–16. Sc into each (54).

Rnd 17. {sc into 8, inc} 6 times (60).

Rnds 18–20. Sc into each (60).

Rnd 21. {sc into 8, dec} 6 times (54).

Rnd 22. {sc into 7, dec} 6 times (48).

Rnd 23. {sc into 6, dec} 6 times (42).

Rnd 24. {sc into 5, dec} 6 times (36).

Add the eyes (see page 126 for guidance).

Rnd 25. {sc into 4, dec} 6 times (30).

Rnd 26. {sc into 3, dec} 6 times (24).

Start to stuff the head.

Rnd 27. {sc into 2, dec} 6 times (18).

Rnd 28. {sc, dec} 6 times (12).

Continue to stuff the head firmly.

Rnd 29. Sc into each FLO (12).

Do not fasten off, continue with the body.

BODY

Rnd 1. {sc, inc} 6 times (18).

Change to the color of the shirt.

Rnd 2. BLO {sc into 2, inc} 6 times (24).

Rnd 3. BLO sc into each (24).

Rnd 4. BLO {sc into 3, inc} 6 times (30).

Rnd 5. BLO sc into each (30).

Rnd 6. BLO {sc into 4, inc} 6 times (36).

Rnd 7. BLO sc into each (36).

Rnd 8. BLO sc into each (36).

Change to the skin color, but before you continue, make the collar using the color of the shirt.

SHIRT COLLAR

Turn the doll upside down and join the white yarn with a sl st to a back loop of round 1 at the center back of the body. Work {(sc, dc, sc) into same st, sl st into next} 9 times. Fasten off and weave in the ends.

Continue crocheting the body:

Rnd 9. Sc into each BLO (36).

Rnds 10–12. Sc into each (36).

Rnd 13. {sc into 16, dec} 2 times (34).

Rnds 14–15. Sc into each (34).

Do not fasten off, continue with the legs. Stuff the neck and body continuously.

LEGS

To make the legs, divide the work: 14 stitches for each of the legs, and 3 stitches between the legs, both front and back. Mark the stitches with yarn or a stitch marker. Make sure the legs line up with the eyes. If the last stitch of the body is within the 14 stitches for the legs, then continue crocheting. If it is within the 3 stitches, then fasten off, leave a tail for sewing later, and rejoin the skin-colored yarn with a sl st at the back of the doll.

Rnds 1–3. Sc into each (14).

Rnd 4. {sc into 5, dec} 2 times (12).

Rnds 5–8. Sc into each (12).

Stuff the body firmly and stuff the leg as you crochet it.

Rnd 9. {sc into 4, dec} 2 times (10).

Rnds 10–12. Sc into each (10).

Stuff the leg firmly.

Rnd 13. Dec 5 times (5).

Fasten off, sew up the small hole, and weave in the ends. For the second leg, rejoin with a sl st at the back of the doll and work the leg. When finished, sew up the hole between the legs. Weave in the ends.

EYEBROWS AND NOSE

Using black thread, embroider the eyebrows between rounds 12 and 14. With skin-colored yarn, embroider the nose between rounds 18 and 19.

SKIRT

Use the light green yarn (to match the hat) for the contrast edging. Join with a sl st to a front loop of round 8 at the center back of the body. Work continuously, but join with a sl st at the end of each round. Ch 1 at the beginning does not count as sc. Work each sc in an "X" shape (see page 122) until the skirt is complete, or use standard sc if you prefer.

Rnd 1. Sl st into each (36). Change to dark green.

Rnd 2. Ch 1, sc into each BLO (36).

Rnd 3. Ch 1, {sc, inc} 18 times (54).

Rnds 4–14. Ch 1, sc into each (54).

Change to light green.

Rnd 15. Sl st into each.

Fasten off and weave in ends.

SHOES

Use the color of the shoes, make two.

Rnd 1. Ch 4, 2 sc into 2nd ch from hook, sc, 3 sc into next. Continue working on the other side of the foundation chain: sc, 2 sc into last (9).

Rnd 2. Inc 2 times, sc, inc 3 times, sc, inc 2 times (16).

Rnd 3. Sc into each BLO (16).

Rnd 4. Sc into 5, dec 3 times, sc into 5 (13).

Rnd 5. Sc into 6, dec, sc into 5 (12).

Fasten off and leave a long tail for sewing. Add stuffing to the toe of the shoes, position them on the legs, and sew them into place. Weave in the ends.

COAT

Start with the dark green yarn. Work in rows, turning at the end of each row. Ch 1 at the beginning does not count as sc.

Row 1. Ch 21, sc into 2nd ch from hook and next 19, turn (20).

Row 2. Ch 1, sc into 2, {inc, sc into 4} 3 times, inc, sc into 2, turn (24).

Row 3. Ch 1, sc into each, turn (24).

Row 4. Sc into 2, {inc, sc into 5} 3 times, inc, sc into 3, turn (28).

Row 5. Sc into each, turn (28).

Row 6. Sc, {inc, sc into 4} 5 times, inc, sc into last, turn (34).

Rows 7–9. Sc into each, turn (34).

Row 10. Sc, {inc, sc into 5} 5 times, inc, sc into 2, turn (40).

Rows 11–12. Sc into each, turn (40).

Change to light green.

Row 13. Sl st into each, turn (40).

Do not fasten off. Ch 1 and continue crocheting sc evenly up the front edge of the coat. Crochet 2 sc into the corner, then continue along the top of the coat. Crochet 2 sc into the other corner and then crochet sc evenly down the other front edge of the coat. Join with a sl st in the first st of row 13. Fasten off and weave in the ends. Fold the upper part of the coat to form a collar and place it onto the body of the doll. Secure it with pins and use small stitches on both sides to sew it into place.

ARMS

Start with the skin color, make two.

Rnd 1. 6 sc into magic ring (6).

Rnd 2. {sc, inc} 3 times (9).

Rnd 3. Sc into each (9).

Rnd 4. {sc into 2, dec} 2 times, sc into last (7).

Change to the dark green coat yarn.

Rnds 5–12. Sc into each (7).

Fasten off and leave a long tail for sewing. Position an arm on each side of the doll and sew them into place.

HAIR

Use the hair color.

Rnd 1. 6 sc into magic ring (6).

Rnd 2. 2 sc into each (12).

Rnd 3. {sc, inc} 6 times (18).

Rnd 4. {sc into 2, inc} 6 times (24).

Rnd 5. {sc into 3, inc} 6 times (30).

Rnd 6. {sc into 4, inc} 6 times (36).

Rnd 7. {sc into 5, inc} 6 times (42).

Rnd 8. {sc into 6, inc} 6 times (48).

Rnd 9. {sc into 7, inc} 6 times (54).

Rnds 10–17. Sc into each (54).

Rnd 18. Dc into 25, hdc into next, sl st into next 2, hdc into next, dc into last 25 (54).

Fasten off and leave a long tail for sewing. Place the hair on the head, secure it with pins, and sew it into place.

BUN

Use the hair color.

Rnd 1. Ch 4, 2 sc into 2nd ch from hook, sc, 3 sc into next. Continue working on the other side of the foundation chain: sc into last 2 (8).

Rnd 2. Inc 2 times, sc, inc 3 times, sc, inc (14).

Rnd 3. Inc 3 times, sc into 4, inc 3 times, sc into 4 (20).

Rnd 4. {sc, inc} 3 times, sc into 4, {sc, inc} 3 times, sc into 4 (26).

Rnd 5. Sc, {sc, inc} 3 times, sc into 7, {sc, inc} 3 times, sc into 6 (32).

Rnds 6–8. Sc into each (32).

Rnd 9. Sc into 6, sl st into next.

Fasten off and leave a long tail for sewing. Stuff the bun, then place it on the head between rounds 9 and 18 of the hair. Secure the bun with pins, stuff it, and sew it into place.

HAT

Use the light green hat color.

Rnd 1. 7 sc into magic ring (7).

Rnd 2. 2 sc into each (14).

Rnd 3. {sc, inc} 7 times (21).

Rnd 4. {sc into 2, inc} 7 times (28).

Rnd 5. {sc into 3, inc} 7 times (35).

Rnd 6. {sc into 4, inc} 7 times (42).

Rnd 7. Sc into each (42).

Rnd 8. Sc into each BLO (42).

Rnd 9. {sc into 5, inc} 7 times (49).

Rnds 10–11. Sc into each (49).

Rnd 12. Twisted sc (see page 122) into each (49).

Join with a sl st to the first st of round 12. Fasten off and weave in the ends. Place the hat on the hair above the bun. Secure it with a few stitches.

FLOWER

Use the flower color.

Rnd 1. 5 sc into magic ring (5). Join with sl st to first sc.

Rnd 2. {ch 1, 2 hdc into same st, ch 1, sl st into same st, sl st into next} 5 times.

Fasten off and leave a long tail for sewing. Sew the flower onto the right side of the hair.

GLASSES

Take the floral wire and find a round object to use to form the ring shape for the glasses. I used the plastic part of a thread spool, with a ½" (1.5 cm) diameter. Wrap the longer end of the wire around the spool, leaving 1½" (4 cm) on the shorter end. Wrap the wire all the way around the spool. For the other ring of the glasses, measure 1¾" (4.5 cm) from the first ring on the longer end of the wire and wrap it around the spool again. Use the spool to shape the curved bridge of the glasses. Bend the stems at right angles and place the glasses on the doll. Insert the stems into the head four stitches away from the eyes between rounds 16 and 17, below the hair.

TECHNIQUES

Even experienced crocheters need to have their memories jogged from time to time. Whether you're a relative beginner or have been crocheting for years, these pages provide a handy reference guide for how to do the essential crochet stitches and techniques for the projects in this book.

CROCHET ABBREVIATIONS

The abbreviations below are used throughout the patterns in the book:

BLO   back loop only
bpdc   back-post double crochet
ch   chain
dc   double crochet
dec   decrease(ing)
FLO   front loop only
fpdc   front-post double crochet
hdc   half double crochet
inc   increase(ing)
prev   previous
rnd(s)   round(s)
sc   single crochet
sk   skip
sl st(s) slip stitch(es)
st(s)   stitch(es)

GAUGE AND PROJECT SIZING

For each of the projects, I used a 2.5 mm crochet hook, and Scheepjes Catona 100% Cotton Mercerized yarn in various colors. With this pairing, the sitting dolls are approximately 6 inches / 15 cm, and the standing ones are 7 inches / 18 cm tall.

If you prefer different yarn brands, feel free to crochet with those, but I suggest using 100% cotton yarn. With Catona yarn to give a 1" x 1" (2.5 cm x 2.5 cm) square, I crocheted 7 single crochet with 8 rounds. I achieved this gauge by crocheting in rounds.

Measurements will change depending on the hook size and yarn you use. If you use thicker yarn with a bigger crochet hook, the doll becomes taller. And the same way, if you use thinner yarn with a smaller crochet hook, the finished doll will be smaller.

STARTING AND FINISHING

Crochet can be worked in rows, beginning with a foundation chain, or in rounds, working outward from a foundation ring of chain stitches or a magic ring.

MAKING A SLIPKNOT

Almost every piece of crochet begins with a slipknot.
1. Make a yarn loop, as pictured.
2. Insert the crochet hook, as shown.
3. Gently pull on the short and long ends of yarn while holding the hook to create a slipknot.

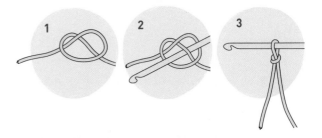

CHAIN STITCH (CH) / FOUNDATION CHAIN

1. Make a slipknot, as shown above. Holding the hook with the slipknot in your right hand and the yarn in your left hand, wrap the yarn over the hook and draw it through the loop.
2. This makes a new loop on the hook and completes the first chain stitch.
3. Repeat this process, drawing a new loop of yarn through the loop already on the hook until the foundation chain is the required length. Count each V-shaped loop on the front of the chain as one chain stitch, except for the loop on the hook, which is not counted.

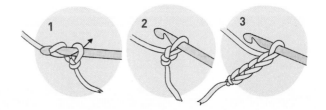

SLIP STITCH (SL ST)

1. Insert the hook in the designated stitch, wrap the yarn over the hook, and pull a new loop through both the work and the loop on the hook. One slip stitch (sl st) made.

2. Repeat Step 1 in each stitch to the end to complete one row of slip stitches.

MAGIC RING

1. Start by making a loop in the yarn, as pictured. Insert the hook into the loop, following the direction of the arrow.

2. Hook the working yarn (the long end) and pull it through the loop, as pictured.

3. Make one chain stitch (or more, if directed by the pattern).

4. Crochet the desired number of stitches into the center of the loop.

5. Pull on the short yarn end to close the center of the magic ring.

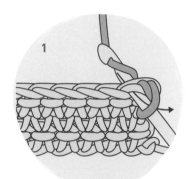

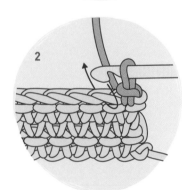

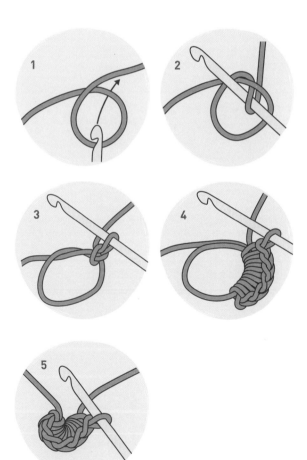

FOUNDATION RING

1. Work a short length of foundation chain as specified in the pattern. Join the chains into a ring by working a slip stitch into the first chain.

2. Work the first round of stitches into the center of the ring unless specified otherwise. At the end of the round, use a slip stitch to join the final stitch to the first stitch if instructed to do so in the pattern.

Weaving in yarn

To weave in a yarn end along the top or lower edge of a piece of crochet, start by threading the end into a yarn or tapestry needle. Take the needle through several stitches on the wrong side of the crochet, working stitch by stitch. Trim the remaining yarn.

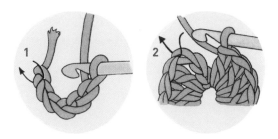

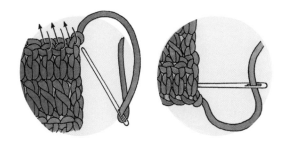

FASTENING OFF AND WEAVING IN ENDS

It is very easy to fasten off yarn when you have finished a piece of crochet, but do not cut the yarn too close to the work because you need enough yarn to weave in the end. It is important to weave in yarn ends securely so that they do not unravel. Do this as neatly as possible so that the woven yarn does not show through on the front of the work.

Fastening off

To fasten off the yarn securely, cut the yarn at least 4" (10 cm) away from the work, and pull the tail through the remaining loop on the hook, tightening it gently.

BASIC STITCHES

SINGLE CROCHET (SC)

1. Insert the hook in the designated stitch, wrap the yarn over the hook, and pull a new loop through this stitch only.

2. Wrap the yarn over the hook, and then pull a loop through both loops on the hook.

3. One loop remains on the hook. One single crochet stitch (sc) made. Repeat Steps 1–2 in each stitch to the end to complete one row of single crochet stitches.

HALF DOUBLE CROCHET (HDC)

1. Wrap the yarn over the hook and insert the hook in the designated stitch.

2. Pull a loop through this stitch. You now have three loops on the hook. Wrap the yarn over the hook again. Pull through all three loops on the hook.

3. One loop remains on the hook. One half double crochet stitch (hdc) made. Repeat Steps 1–2 in each stitch to the end to complete one row of half double crochet stitches.

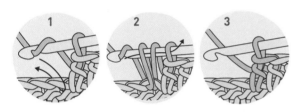

DOUBLE CROCHET (DC)

1. Wrap the yarn over the hook and insert the hook in the designated stitch.

2. Pull a loop through this stitch to make three loops on the hook. Wrap the yarn over the hook again. Pull a new loop through the first two loops on the hook, as pictured. Two loops remain on the hook. Wrap the yarn over the hook again. Pull a new loop through both remaining loops on the hook.

3. One double crochet stitch (dc) made. Repeat Steps 1–2 in each stitch to the end to complete one row of double crochet stitches.

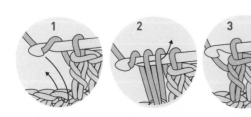

BASIC STITCH VARIATIONS

SINGLE CROCHET (SC) IN AN "X" SHAPE

You can achieve this look if you wrap the yarn under the crochet hook instead of wrapping it over.

1. Insert the hook in the designated stitch. Wrap the yarn under the hook and pull a loop through to make two loops on the hook.

2. Wrap the yarn under the hook again and pull a loop through both loops on the hook. One loop remains on the hook. One single crochet in an "X" shape made.

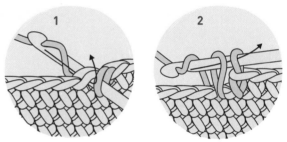

TWISTED SINGLE CROCHET

1. Insert the hook from front to back in the designated stitch. Wrap the yarn over the hook and pull a loop through the stitch to make two loops on the hook. Try to keep the loops loose.

2. With two loops on the hook, rotate the hook counterclockwise by 360 degrees.

3. Wrap the yarn over the hook again and pull a loop through both loops on the hook. One twisted single crochet stitch made.

WORKING INTO ONE LOOP ONLY

If the hook is inserted under just one loop at the top of a stitch, the empty loop creates a ridge on either the front or the back of the fabric. "Front loop only" means the loop nearest to you, at the top of the stitch, and "back loop only" means the farther loop, whether you are working a right-side or a wrong-side row.

Front loop only (FLO)

If the hook is inserted under the front loop only, the empty back loop will show as a ridge on the other side of the work.

Back loop only (BLO)

If the hook is inserted under the back loop only, the empty front loop creates a ridge on the side of the work facing you. These examples show single crochet.

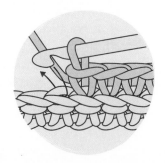

POST STITCHES

These are created by inserting the hook around the post of a stitch below—from the front or back—and are a great way to add texture to your crochet work. Front post stitches are slightly raised and back post stitches slightly recede. The two examples shown here are the front post double crochet (fpdc) and the back post double crochet (bpdc), which are the most common— but most regular stitches can be worked as front or back post stitches. The only thing that sets them apart is where they are worked.

Front post double crochet (fpdc)

1. Wrap the yarn over the hook. Inserting the hook through the work from front to back, take it from right to left around the post of the specified stitch below and then bring it through to the front again.

2. Wrap the yarn over the hook and pull through to make three loops on the hook. Wrap the yarn over again and pull through two loops on the hook. Wrap the yarn over once more and pull through both loops on the hook. So, you complete the stitch as you would a regular dc. A ridge forms on the other side of the work.

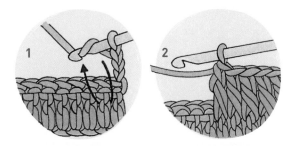

Back post double crochet (bpdc)

1. Wrap the yarn over the hook. Inserting the hook through the work from back to front, take it from right to left around the post of the specified stitch below and then take it through to the back again.

2. Complete as you would a regular dc, as explained in Step 2 of front post double crochet. A ridge forms on the side of the work facing you.

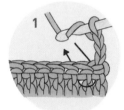

SPECIAL STITCHES

INCREASING AND DECREASING

Shaping in amigurumi is made by increasing (and decreasing) stitches, which means working two or more single crochet into the same stitch.

Working several stitches in the same place

This technique is used to increase the total number of stitches in a row or round. Increases may be worked at the edges of flat pieces, or at any point along a row. Two, three, or more stitches may be worked into the same place to make a fan of stitches, often called a shell.

Invisible decrease

Insert the hook into the front loop of the next two stitches and pull a loop through both. Wrap the yarn over the hook and pull through the last two loops on the hook.

POPCORN STITCH

A popcorn is a group of stitches worked in the same place and then folded and closed at the top so that the popcorn is raised from the background stitches. Work the specified number of stitches in the same place. Take the hook out of the working loop and insert it under both top loops of the first stitch of the popcorn. Pick up the working loop with the hook and draw it through to fold the group of stitches and close the popcorn at the top.

TECHNIQUES

CHANGING COLORS

Use this method for a neat join between colors. The first ball need not be fastened off; it may be left aside for a few rows or stitches in the course of a multicolored pattern.
1. Work up to the final "yarn over, pull through" of the last stitch in the old color and wrap the new color around the hook.
2. Use the new color to complete the stitch.
3. Continue in the new color.

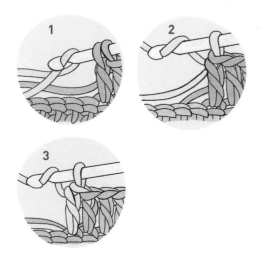

JOINING ROUNDS WITH A SLIP STITCH

Most amigurumi patterns are worked in continuous rounds without joins, but some pattern pieces require you to make a slip stitch join to the first stitch of the round, as shown.

JOINING PARTS

Crochet pieces may be seamed with a tapestry needle. Use the same yarn as used for the main pieces, if possible. If this is too bulky, choose a matching, finer yarn, preferably with the same fiber content to avoid problems when the article is washed.

Backstitch seam

This is a firm seam that resists stretching. Hold the pieces with right sides together (pin them if necessary, as shown), matching the stitches or row ends, and use a tapestry needle and matching yarn to work backstitches, as shown.

Woven seam

This seam is flexible and flat. Lay the pieces with edges touching, wrong sides up, and use a tapestry needle and matching yarn to weave around the centers of the edge stitches, as shown. Do not pull the stitches too tightly; the seam should stretch as much as the work itself. When joining row ends, work in a similar way.

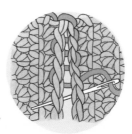

STUFFING

If you are using a loose filling such as polyester fiberfill, it is best to stuff as you go. This is easier than trying to poke the stuffing through a small opening at the end.

Take small amounts of stuffing and pull the fibers apart before placing in the doll. As more stuffing is placed inside, ensure that it reaches the edges and corners. You can prevent lumps by continuously filling rather than having breaks in the fiber.

If the stuffing becomes lumpy or starts clumping together, pull it out and start over. To ensure an even distribution, use the blunt end of a knitting needle or chopstick to move the stuffing around until you are happy.

EYES

Most of the dolls in the book have $5/16$" (8 mm) safety eyes—except for Bruce Lee, where $5/16$" (8 mm) oval safety eyes are used. However, If you make any of the dolls for children under the age of three, you might want to embroider the eyes for safety reasons. You can add them at the same stage that you embroider the eyebrows and nose.

If you are using safety eyes, cut two circles—a little larger than the safety eyes—from the white felt and make holes in the middle of the circles. Place the safety eyes into the holes. Insert them between rounds 17 and 18, with ten stitches between the eyes. Place the eyes on the opposite side to the start of the round.

EMBROIDERY

The facial features and other embroidered details are worked using backstitch. This stitch is useful for creating outlining and lines.

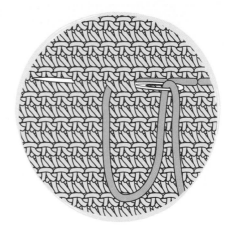

Bring the needle through from the back of the work. From the front and in one motion, take the needle through to the back a short distance along to the right, then draw it through the work to the front the same distance along to the left from the beginning of the stitch. Continue from right to left by inserting the needle through from front to back at the point where the last stitch emerged.

INDEX

ACKNOWLEDGMENTS

Firstly, I would like to thank my family for making this book possible. I never pictured writing a book, but to create one during this unprecendented year has been beyond imagination. I am thankful to my husband for helping me in many ways, for occupying our children, and even giving great tips on Prince. I also thank my brother for the great insights into the life of the amazing athletes I crocheted for this book.

I'd like to thank the lovely team at Quarto Publishing. To Eszter for finding me, to Kate for trusting me with this idea, to Emma for coordinating and helping me through this process, and to Martina for making the book look this beautiful. I'm thankful to you all for being so patient with my constant worrying. This book is a dream come true for me.

I'm grateful to all of the heroes I chose to crochet. Each and everyone of them has taught me something meaningful during these challenging times.

And last but not least, thank you to my dear Manuska crochet friends and family around the world. Your kind words, encouragement, and constant support in our wonderful digital social space mean the world to me.